Hurry Less Worry Less at Work

Hurry Less Worry Less at Work

JUDY CHRISTIE

Abingdon Press
Nashville

HURRY LESS, WORRY LESS AT WORK

This book is printed on acid-free paper.

Library of Congress Cataloging-in-Publication Data

Christie, Judy Pace, 1956–
Hurry less, worry less at work / Judy Christie.
p. cm.
ISBN 978-0-687-65783-4 (pbk. : alk. paper)
1. Simplicity—Religious aspects—Christianity. 2. Time management—Religious aspects—Christianity. 3. Work—Religious aspects—Christianity.
I. Title.
BV4647.S48C47 2009
241'.64—dc22

2009021996

09 10 11 12 13 14 15 16 17 18 — 10 9 8 7 6 5 4 3 2 1

MANUFACTURED IN THE UNITED STATES OF AMERICA

To my brothers,

Jack, Steve, and David

CONTENTS

With Gratitude

The generosity and perspective of a large number of people helped me write this book—friends, family, clients, and colleagues who were willing to ponder tough questions and provide thought-provoking ideas. Each of you knows who you are and will see your thoughts reflected in these pages. I offer deep appreciation to you. God has blessed you with wisdom, and you share it faithfully—in how you live your daily lives and how you serve others.

Very special thanks go to my early coaches—friends Alisa Stingley, Kathie Rowell, Rita Hummingbird, and Ginger Hamilton—for their feedback and keen brains; Pastor Rob Weber, Barbara Montgomery, Pete Bollinger, my small group, and the rest of my church family at Grace Community United Methodist Church, who will see themselves woven throughout this book; my dear Baylor Funfest Friends; June Foster and my other neighbors at Colony House of Flowers, who encouraged me as I wrote; granddaughter Gracie, who brought many smiles as this book was wrapped up; and my agent, Etta Wilson, a wonderful teacher and friend.

And, finally, once more, loving thanks to my husband, Paul, who lets me try out all sorts of hurry less, worry less ideas and always cheers me on.

Introduction

I urge you to live a life worthy of the calling you have received. —Ephesians 4:1

As a teenager, I begged my mother to let me get a job. Going to work seemed glamorous—a way to ease summer boredom or an excuse to buy new clothes. The thought of earning spending money was appealing. My mother, herself a hard worker who supported our family, discouraged me. "You'll be working the rest of your life," she said. "Don't rush into it."

In the years since, I have discovered that work is a very full and challenging part of my life. I wrestle on a daily basis with colliding priorities, most of which involve my career. My goal is to enjoy each day, living abundantly—and that means knowing when to focus on work, when to leave the job behind, and how to blend my personal and professional lives. I need God's guidance in my daily work life as much as anywhere, probably *more* than anywhere. Divine help is required to know what I was created for and to make the best use of my time and energy.

God has something for each of us to do that suits no one else in quite the same way. We are not put on earth merely to get by but to live to the fullest. We must guard against planning to be happy "somewhere down the road," being dismayed at our current lives, or thinking we will do such-and-such after we retire. God calls us to live joyfully, here and now. That call must shape our work—whether it's a full-time paying job or a demanding volunteer role or a combination of both.

From my teen years on, I have had interesting jobs, some positions that paid well and some that paid little, working for others and for myself, doing basic tasks and carrying out executive responsibilities. Many times I have had to remind myself to try to be worthy of the calling I have received—and to keep that as a priority. Enjoying work more—as part of a rich, blessed life—is an ongoing process that involves hundreds of daily decisions and much prayer. Course corrections are needed regularly.

After my first book, *Hurry Less, Worry Less: 10 Strategies for Living the Life You Long For*, was published, people told me they longed for a better approach to work. Many liked their jobs but felt too rushed. Others had drifted into vocations that did not seem right for them. Most wondered how to balance home and employment. This book unfolded from those conversations and my own tug-of-war.

Our work—whatever it is—can be of service to God, *must* be of service to God. We are called, always, to love and serve through our daily lives, and that includes in our jobs. Take hope! You can make needed changes—large and small.

Blending work and home is similar to undertaking a repair job around the house. The right tools must be in the toolbox, and you need to know what you are trying to accomplish. Then you choose a tool and put it to use. This is where many of us falter, knowing what to do but not doing it. At other times, we are confused, needing instructions spelled out. Slowing down, becoming even better at your work and enjoying each day takes daily attention.

My desire is for this book to provide you with practical skills and inspirational ideas—offering the right tools for your "repair project," including trust in God as the divine architect to shape your work life. To help you make any needed changes, chapters include questions and simple steps to consider, tips from real people who struggle with these challenges, and prayers for your journey. You will also find many scriptures whose old truths speak to modern dilemmas. A chapter-by-chapter study guide, which can be used individually or with a group, is located at the back of the book and offers questions to take you further on your way. For remarkable results, please take time in your busy life to do the exercises throughout the book. Praying, studying, and writing down ideas can keep you moving forward and offer new insights. Digging deeper is not particularly easy, but God speaks through such efforts.

You can learn to enjoy each day more—to be content with work; to learn and grow at your job; to serve others through your career; to rest, relax, and renew.

Take a deep breath, and prepare to change your approach to work.

"The LORD bless you / and keep you; / the LORD make his face shine upon you / and be gracious to you; / the LORD turn his face toward you / and give you peace" (Numbers 6:24-26).

Chapter One

Too Much Work, Too Little Time

Learning to Enjoy Each Day More

Encouraging Word: *You can make your work dreams come true.*
Everyday Step: *Take a fresh look at your life.*

You are not here merely to make a living. You are here in order to enable the world to live more amply, with greater vision, with a finer spirit of hope and achievement. You are here to enrich the world, and you impoverish yourself if you forget the errand. —*Woodrow Wilson*

A varied group of people gathered with me for a night course about living more positively. The members were different in many ways, but a thread ran through their stories: everyone in this group had a demanding job. During our few evenings together, cell phones of every kind tried to intrude, and work issues took members out of the room regularly.

This wonderful class was made up of people with interesting and useful work. Their professional activities were downright inspirational—from help in hospice care and with cancer treatment to high-school administration and a focus on homeless people. The members were deeply committed to their families and were trying to grow as part of a church community.

But each individual was juggling so much—trying to do well at work, with family issues, with daily logistics, and with finding time for self-care. As I visited with the members of the group, I was reminded again of the importance of stepping back and assessing life and work on a regular basis.

Most people go so fast all the time that they do not take time to consider a different way of living. They feel too bogged down to make changes. Nearly everywhere I go, people talk about how busy they are and how demanding their work is. Some folks love their careers but are overwhelmed by trying to set priorities. Others are worn out and have lost the enjoyment they once got from their jobs.

Many simply have too much work to do and too little time. Some work because they feel they have to—either to make a living or because it is somehow expected of them. Others work because they feel called to do a certain job or want to make a difference in the world. Most of the people I have encountered work for a combination of the two—money to support their lifestyle or their daily needs *and* to do something meaningful.

Our motivation to work often starts with the right reason—perhaps it's a job we really love or we are happy to get—but that reason can get lost in the hectic pace of daily life. This reminds me of my young granddaughter when she gets going too fast on her bicycle. She begins to swerve all over the place and then makes a less-than-graceful stop. Instead of moderating her speed and regaining control, she crashes.

People who want to slow down at work tend to take this same approach. They go so fast they crash—through job burnout, relationship problems, or a health issue. *Then* they are sometimes willing to slow down and assess their situation. However, often before long, they find themselves out of control again.

A better way is to start today taking inventory of your work life and see what changes you want to make. This awareness will spill over into all areas of your life and will be a catalyst for amazing things. When you hurry less and worry less at work, you will notice a ripple effect.

For years now I have worked with busy people on learning to handle this issue. A good tried-and-true first step is to take a fresh look at your life and work. You need a new perspective in order to make important decisions and to use simple tools to change. Like my granddaughter, you may be going too fast and in danger of a crash, but you can still get your "bicycle" under control.

For encouragement, remember all of the great people in the Bible—everyday, working people. They were carpenters and tentmakers and fishermen. Work played a part in their lives—but only a part. They used it to complement the people they were created to be.

Making needed changes does not mean quitting your job or becoming slothful at work or ignoring the need for money to buy groceries. Change can mean adding more effective practices to your daily work, getting more done in less time, fretting less, and listening closely to make sure you are where you are supposed to be.

Start Praying About Your Work, Expecting God to Guide You

In my own efforts to slow down and enjoy work more, I found myself resisting God's guidance, wanting to get my own daily messiness straightened up first. My overloaded calendar and disorganized desk screamed for attention.

God was more subtle.

Somewhere along the way, I realized God wanted to help me, wanted good things for me, and did *not* want me to be rushing around in an on-the-job dither. Nor did the Lord want me to neglect other important parts of my life in the name of my career.

Even more noticeable was the need to involve God in each step of this journey and to avoid thinking I would handle some of it on my own and then turn to God for more-spiritual or important efforts.

Without prayer and God's help, the calm, meaningful life we want slams up against a turbocharged schedule and a mile-long to-do list. Our personal lives, professional lives, and spiritual lives cannot be separated. They are the strands that make up who we are—and one does not work without the other. Great peace and contentment await us when we begin to figure that out.

A favorite scripture speaks directly of this: "Do not conform any longer to the pattern of this world, but be transformed by the renewing of your mind. Then you will be able to test and approve what God's will is—his good, pleasing and perfect will" (Romans 12:2). As you consider changes, ponder this verse. Stepping back can help renew your mind—and it can lead you to the place where you are supposed to be.

Consider These "ABCs" of Getting and Staying on Track

Assess. This tool is often overlooked by busy people. We get so rushed that we fail to set aside time for the important process of figuring out *what* we want our lives to look like and *how* we are going to achieve our goals. Set aside at least a few hours to take a snapshot of where your life and career are and to develop a plan to get yourself where you want to be.

Believe that you can live the life you long for. I see lots of people who are just getting by each day because they do not believe they can make needed changes. Decide that you can achieve dreams, do things you have longed to do, hurry and worry less.

Change as needed. Most people don't care much for change—we like the way things are. I encounter some who say, "That's the way we've always done it" or "We tried that, and it doesn't work." Maybe now is the time to make changes in your job—either with the work you do altogether or in your daily routine. Or maybe you merely need to change your attitude about work.

Next, **deliver**. We are called to deliver something back to the world, to make it a better place because we walked through our corner of it. As you rethink your priorities, consider what you are doing with the gifts you've been given. Most of us, even on our worst days, have more gifts than many others in the world. You don't have to have all the answers or be a saint to make a huge difference each day, wherever you are, whoever you are. Our world desperately needs kind and generous people who are willing to roll up their sleeves and get their hands dirty, people who live by the Golden Rule, treating others as they want to be treated.

Finally, **enjoy each day**. Children typically look forward and laugh and have fun. As we get older, often we tend to look more at the negative side of life. Look for the good in each day. Give thanks for the blessings that surround you. Have some fun.

While these ABCs are simple, they are not always easy. Each person is different, and the challenges of work and life vary. However, you can make customized changes suited for you. As you move forward, remember that God blazes the way for you: "The LORD your God, who is going before you, will fight for you" (Deuteronomy 1:30). With a holy Guidance Counselor, just imagine what can happen.

Use the Gift of Prayer

Begin with prayer. If you aren't accustomed to praying on a regular basis, do not be overwhelmed. Prayer is simply communicating with God. Start now, asking God to guide you as you attempt to slow down. Reflect upon what God wants your life to look like. Ask to be transformed—changed from within and in your daily actions as needed. Seek the Lord's perfect will.

The Bible clearly tells us to call upon God for everything, that the Lord is interested in our daily lives: "Here is my servant, whom I uphold, my chosen one in whom I delight" (Isaiah 42:1). God, through great love, delights in us and upholds us. As Jesus said, "I have come that they may have life, and have it to the full" (John 10:10). This is what God wants for us—abundant life.

Since work plays such an important part in our daily lives, we need to find ways to enjoy it, to see our work as a blessing and to use our gifts to make a difference. How can we possibly live fully if we do not learn how to deal with the daily busyness?

Refresh the Big Picture for Your Life

Pondering the Big Picture is a rewarding exercise that can help you renew hope and put away regrets. This can help in the days ahead when you must take care of nitty-gritty details.

Thank God for your past—warts and all—knowing it has helped you in many ways. Ask for help in the future—a season that can be quite inviting. Tinker a bit or make wholesale changes, covered by God's love. Knowing that God has a perfect, customized will for your life is energizing. While it may not be totally clear to you each and every day, you can always know its core: love God, and love others as you love yourself.

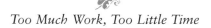

For many people, work is a huge part of the Big Picture. Our job is often our calling, the way we are created to serve. Our Big Picture needs to reflect this—but it also needs to include other important components, such as family and volunteer efforts.

You may have an uneasy feeling such as I had several years back, when I knew I needed to do things differently but I wasn't sure what shape this might take. Begin to look a little deeper, and pray for God's help in this process.

The familiar words of Jeremiah 29:11 are encouraging as you revisit possibilities for your work: " 'For I know the plans I have for you,' declares the LORD, 'plans to prosper you and not to harm you, plans to give you hope and a future.' "

These words reassured me many times as I considered the Big Picture for my life. What a comfort to know that God's plans are for prosperity and safety, a hopeful future. This promise can fortify you when you step back and try to hurry less and worry less. Consideration of life and work is extremely personal, and the road map for your life may be completely different from that of a coworker or friend. Our uniqueness is part of what God has given us and what we give back to the world. Keep this in mind as you ponder changes. "Everyone's situation is a bit different," said a spiritual director and Christian educator with a wise perspective on work-life balance. "Folks have different energy levels, some are more introverted and others more extroverted, family and work dynamics can be quite different, and experiences that can renew one person might bore or stress out someone else."

Ask and Answer Key Questions

Are you familiar with the game Twenty Questions? You may have played it as a child. Someone thinks of a person, place, or thing, and others may ask up to twenty questions as they try to guess the answer. A similar approach can help you establish the Big Picture for your life, set priorities, and help make sure you stay on the path that is right for you.

Give thought to the following twenty questions or come up with your own. Write down your answers and see what bubbles up.

- What am I happiest about in my life?
- What have I accomplished that matters to me?
- Am I using my time and energy in the ways I want?
- What gives me energy?
- What drains my energy?
- How are my relationships?
- Who needs more of my attention?
- Why did I choose the work I now do?
- What is working well in my job?
- What changes do I need to consider in my work?
- Am I taking care of my physical health?
- Do I need to add exercise to my life?
- Am I making time for rest, reflection, and renewal?
- Am I involved in a church where I worship, grow, and give something back?
- Do I serve others at home, in my church, or in my community?

- Is my money situation under control?
- What gifts and talents do I have?
- How can I use those gifts and talents to do and enjoy meaningful work?
- Am I learning in my daily life?
- Do I have fun?

Some of these questions are easy to answer. Others require more thought. Do not shy away from asking hard questions to come up with revealing answers about your priorities and how well you are honoring those. This simple process can lead to better decisions and help you be more effective at work. Answering these questions can provide insight into how you are spending the precious days you have been given.

"We are not accidents or coincidences," said a Louisiana attorney. "Each of us has been created by God to fulfill part of his purpose on earth. That means we are not put here to play, although he does want us to enjoy his gifts. Jesus was a party guy, but he didn't live to party. He lived to serve."

This same lawyer tells of his challenge in shaping a vision with service to God and love for his family: "My professional life is a calling for me. The struggle for me has been to reach some balance between my calling and the needs of my family. I believe I am serving God by being a good lawyer and counselor for my clients. God has given me such grace and mercy that I have tried to extend grace and mercy to others."

"The Ability to Step Back"

Another professional mentions the importance of God's part in our Big Picture: "It all begins with focusing on what we're called to do on this earth, all of us." That, along with stepping back to reshape his vision on a regular basis, helps him keep priorities in order. "One of the gifts God gave me is the ability to step back," he said, stressing the importance of relying on the life of Christ as a model for work. "That will lead you to the right priorities. To be a workaholic, compulsive, impulsive is not what you want."

God sometimes lays projects out right before us, perhaps showing problems that need our gifts to be solved. As a consultant, I appreciate the biblical story of Nehemiah, who had a good job with the king but was troubled by something he felt called to do. We read how God used this man to help rebuild the walls—and thus change the heart—of the city of Jerusalem. As an Old Testament "consultant," he saw a problem and knew that his help was needed.

Nehemiah was quite afraid, though, when he went to the king, just like many of us are when we face new challenges. So Nehemiah prayed, and he took the challenge anyway, giving up his prestigious position because he felt God calling him. When Nehemiah traveled to Jerusalem to get the project going, he said, "The God of heaven will give us success" (Nehemiah 2:20). He had been troubled by something, prayed about it, and set out, certain he was exactly where God wanted him to be. Nehemiah had vision and faith, and he did the hard work required to accomplish his task.

Perhaps you have followed your early dreams or a calling throughout the years. Or maybe you changed your mind at a later time and found something even better for you. Possibly you let time and situations wear you down and extinguish some of those "what if" possibilities.

No matter your age, dust off your youthful perspective and see what it says to you about the work you are doing. Recall what excited you on your youthful thresholds, what you felt destined to do, and what you were enthusiastic about.

Contemplate how your life has changed and how that affects the Big Picture you want for your life—and the calling God has for you.

The Picture of Success

Understand there will likely be trade-offs as you try to slow down.

For me, being a newspaper executive and working in the journalism industry at a national level was rewarding for many years—and, I admit, I liked the success. However, when God began to nudge me to make changes, success began to look different. I could not measure it by income and status but by doing each day what I felt God was calling me to do.

A financial advisor with young children has also wrestled with this issue: "The greatest challenge I face is how to define success. The definition changes, at least for me, as the years go by and as I develop into my career. I don't want to be the guy who never appreciates what he has, but at the same time, I want to be the best at what I do. I feel the definition of success must include career, family, physical, mental, and spiritual. I try and set goals for each, define where I want to go, and set my goals with boundaries as well."

Following his process, along with using your answers to the twenty questions outlined earlier, can be a useful tool as you update a vision for your life—both professionally and personally. Make a list of things you want to do, goals you want to accomplish. Make sure there are meaningful career or volunteer activities on that list. To begin to change, remember:

- You have to stop and assess regularly. Determine what you want your work life to be like and how to get there. Figure out the what, and then the how.

- God has a plan for each of us—and that includes the work we choose to do. To live this plan we need to pray, listen, and make changes as needed. Everyday life is not static, and our work life certainly is not, either.
- You can't do everything or be everything. Trim activities from your work schedule, even though this may be tough. Make choices that align work priorities and personal priorities under the umbrella of your Big Picture.
- Work can be especially challenging and difficult in these days of doing more with less and times of change. Most people want to do meaningful work—fantasies about huge inheritances aside!—but can easily get in a rut or find themselves burned out.

Don't make excuses. March right out and give it your best. Learning better ways to handle the busyness of your work is not a quick-and-easy process, but it can be done—even if you feel as though you are mired in an impossible situation.

"May the favor of the Lord our God rest upon us; establish the work of our hands for us—yes, establish the work of our hands" (Psalm 90:17).

Whisper a prayer. Then take a step forward and see what happens.

A PRAYER FOR YOUR JOURNEY

Dear Lord, shape the Big Picture for my life according to your plan. Give me wisdom and courage as I assess my life and consider changes that you would have me make. Help me know how to approach my professional life. In thy name. Amen.

Tips from Busy People

Love what you do.

"It is important to find a vocation you really love. If you can find work that uses your unique gifts and talents and that you find rewarding on most days, that can help a lot."

Have a life outside of work.

"Coming to the realization that I had no life outside the office was one of the hardest things I've ever done. But once the lightbulb came on, I knew that only God could fix it. And he did. I must admit that my life is much happier these days, now that I don't spend as much time at work as I used to do. The key for me was deciding that it was imperative for me to create a life for myself outside of the office."

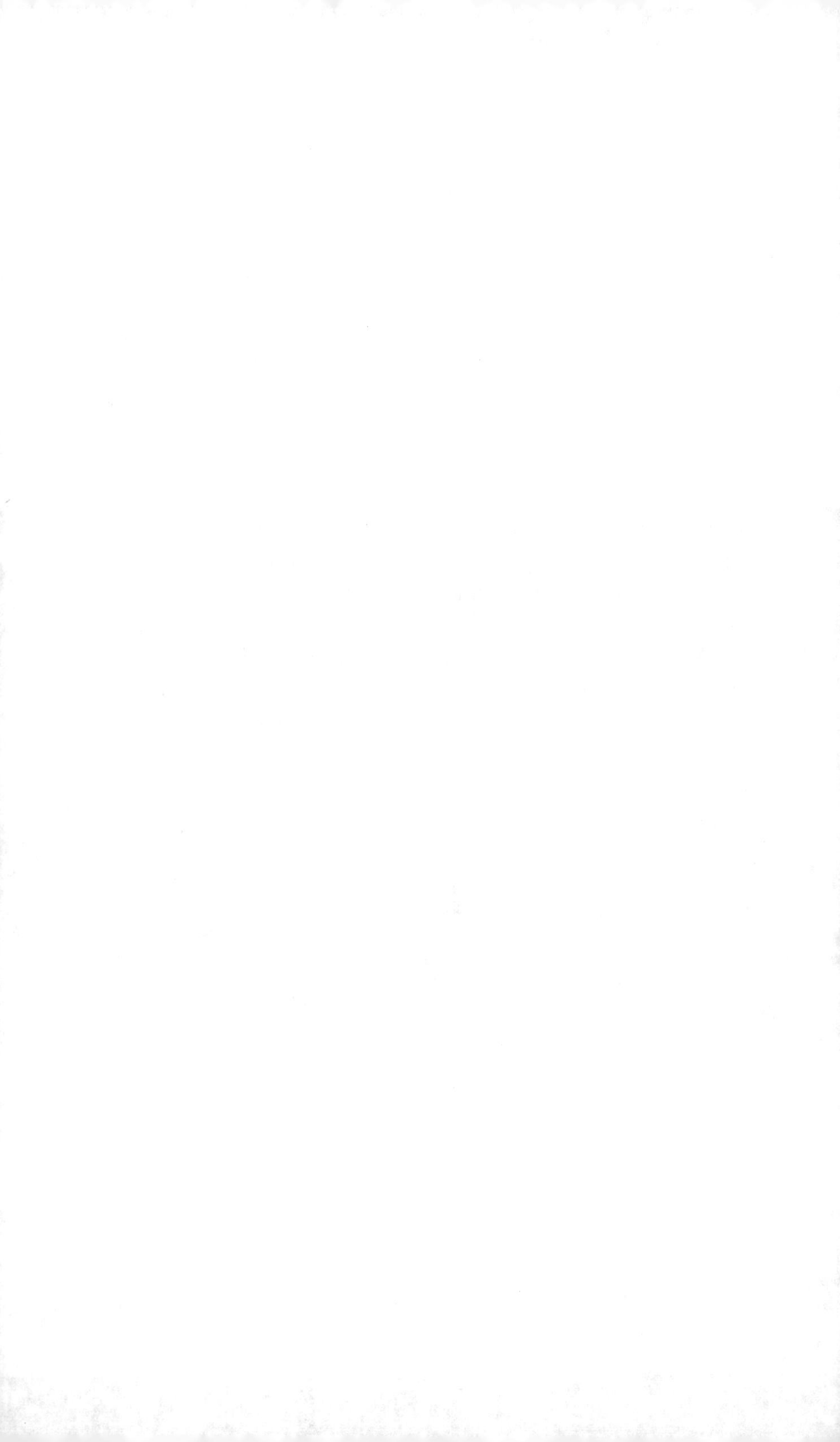

Chapter Two

The Importance of Priorities

Making Daily Decisions

Encouraging Word: *You can spend time on what you love.*
Everyday Step: *Decide to make one simple change at work.*

Action expresses priorities. —Mahatma Gandhi

The batch of graduation invitations piles up each year, with photos of smiling students about to embark on brand-new adventures. These announcements remind me of how fast time flies: *How could that child be old enough to graduate?* They often take me back to those days when anything seemed possible.

We need this reminder as we struggle to balance work and the rest of our lives, identifying our priorities and living by them. Somewhere along the way, many people lose their anticipation about the promise of life—and cease believing that opportunities and adventures are in front of them. We stumble when we do not live each day according to our priorities. We too often go with the flow and are swept away by the demands of each particular day, waking up to see that years have passed and we are not where we want to be.

When I walked out the doors of Byrd High School in Shreveport, Louisiana, and Baylor University in Waco, Texas, I had all sorts of dreams and plans. Some of them worked out just as I imagined. Others required tweaking. Others I abandoned because the time was not right or because I found something else that suited me better. Some I am just now pursuing.

My life has been greatly enriched by stretching and taking calculated chances. Dreaming big dreams makes life much more interesting and just plain fun. Tweaking those dreams keeps me growing. But for all of this to work, I must keep my priorities in mind—knowing that the first priority always is to seek God's plan for my life and follow God's direction.

"There is nothing in a caterpillar that tells you it's going to be a butterfly," said the brilliant Buckminster Fuller (whom I had the privilege of hearing speak in my college days). Just like a caterpillar becoming a butterfly, you may experience an amazing transformation in your own life when you are consistently true to your priorities—a change from within that you did not expect or hope for. I dare you to reassess your path in life, to begin to make needed changes in your work.

See yourself standing up front and center, laying out ideas for how you might proceed, what you might do if you were making a fresh start. Keep your Big Picture in mind. This does not mean throwing away the life you have. Instead, use it as a foundation, making needed changes and keeping other things just as they are. Perhaps you will see that your vision means making a series of changes over a period of time.

Refusing to take a deeper look at work may feel more comfortable, but it is not. You may need to stay put—or perhaps you are too tired, settled, or cautious of rocking the boat to consider new ways of living. Maybe things are secure as they are.

Sometimes people are haunted by the past and are afraid to make changes. We cannot erase the past, even if parts of it are less than stellar, but we can consider what we have learned along the way.

Perhaps you merely need a reminder of why you chose the work you now do in the first place—and how to regain joy you once had.

Focusing on Priorities

As you begin to take inventory of your work life, focus on priorities. To make wise decisions based on priorities, keep your Big Picture in mind. This can prevent you from being drawn off course as you figure out where work fits into your life.

Nearly everyone can rattle off a list of priorities. *Work* is sometimes on that list, occasionally out of a felt necessity rather than a true passion. Usually *family* is there, and sometimes *fitness* or *health*. Often *volunteer efforts* and *church* round out the list.

When you take a closer look, work takes up much of your time, no matter how important it is in your life overall. While many of us need and want to work, we also value time with our families and friends, and time for church and civic activities. Plus, we need time for hobbies, exercise, and rest.

What can you do to keep work from swamping you and throwing other priorities out of whack?

Perhaps you are in a season of time when you want to focus on your career and build income for family needs. Or perhaps work is becoming less of your focus. You have worked for years and are shifting gears. Or it's possible you have reached career goals and find yourself wanting more time to do other things. Maybe you feel God asking you to serve in a special way outside paid work—and, thus, you keep a steady job but don't think about it once the workday is over.

Each of these scenarios involves daily decisions.

Try to make choices in your daily life that support your priorities. Remember that saying no to one thing is really saying yes to something else. Pick your spots wisely.

Write down the hours you have committed each day—getting ready for work, getting to and from work, time at work, meals, getting children up and ready, and so forth. See how much time you have left. This can help you rearrange your priorities and make hard decisions to allow more time for rest and fun.

You cannot do everything. The CEO of a large nonprofit agency in the South uses this philosophy to avoid overload: "I approach balancing personal and professional stuff this way: we all have but one life to live. Every human being has the exact same amount of time to devote to whatever we choose. We each have twenty-four hours a day. Setting priorities is the key. I realize we all get pulled in many directions, but knowing what is important to me is the key to balancing my life."

My Life and My Priorities: Am I on the Right Path to Live with Joy?

Consider what you want to focus on as priorities in your life right now—not when the children are grown or when you retire or when the economy changes. Right now.

List those things—about three or so. Don't make your list too long, because if you have too many priorities, it is impossible to focus on them. Decide what is truly most important in your life and work. Form a clear picture of how you want to spend your time and energy, and this will make it easier to decide what to cut.

Figure out what is nonnegotiable in your life, and use that to shape daily decisions. Perhaps it is a dream you simply will not let go of, such as going back to college, or the time you spend with your family, a commitment to your church, your health, or something altogether different. These nonnegotiables can help us make smart and, sometimes, difficult choices.

Priorities will vary, depending on where you are in life. Perhaps you are relocating or getting married or getting divorced, recovering from an illness, or helping an aging parent. Maybe you will turn down a promotion to spend more time with your young children. Many events shape the choices you make regarding work.

Once you have determined what your priorities are, consider what you need to quit focusing on so much. Perhaps you obsess about work when you are at home, or maybe you find yourself talking negatively about a coworker or your boss. Maybe you fret about what is not right and let that pull you into a glum attitude about work.

Giving Your Best Time and Attention to Top Priorities

When I assessed my priorities a few months ago, I realized I was guilty of what I warn others about—trying to do too much. My schedule was getting overloaded. A new desire was clamoring for attention—the dream of writing more books. I needed to pay more attention to my top priorities, and something had to go. I closed my small, part-time retail shop and turned down a major community volunteer job, both with regret, but knowing I was making the right choices.

Perhaps you find yourself facing that same dilemma in your life. Give your top priorities your best time and attention. Get rid of activities and obligations as needed. Do not be seduced by worthwhile or enticing choices that do not align with your priorities. Do not volunteer to do something simply because it looks good or is interesting. Choose it because it suits what you want and—most important—what you sense God wants for your life and work. Do not forget personal priorities in doing this.

This is a very hard concept for most folks to live by. When it comes to overloading, we seldom choose between bad things and good things. We more likely choose between Good Thing One and Good Thing Two.

"Sometimes I feel very proud of all the things I accomplish, but then other times I feel like I am doing a lot of things but none of them very well," a manager said. "I always have more things I want to get done than time allows. That means I'm always making choices about what *doesn't* get done."

If you are like me and find yourself juggling too many things, perhaps you need to trim a big item from your schedule or make another change that lines up with your priorities. What might you eliminate?

Consider an array of tools to help you honor priorities and move forward in calm and purposeful ways.

Start with Basics Guaranteed to Help, No Matter How Overwhelmed You Feel

As I mentioned earlier, when it comes to repairing your life, prayer is a great tool. Ask God to help you. First

Thessalonians 5:17 tells us to "pray continually." Weave prayer throughout your workday—in those hectic first moments when you awaken and think of all you have to do that day, as you travel to the office, when you walk into your place of work, as you go about your daily duties, and when worries about work keep you awake at night.

"Pray continually."

Another tool is more mundane: a good calendar to keep you on schedule. Keep track of your personal and professional appointments, so you will not be scrambling to reschedule or rushing to reach an activity booked too closely to another. Start on this immediately.

"I discovered the importance of maintaining a calendar, including blocks of time for family, God, study, and renewal," a pastor said. "There will always be unforeseen events and circumstances beyond our control, but approaching these various events and circumstances from a place of balance allows for a more stable response and an easier return to the regular rhythm of a balanced life."

A journal can be incredibly handy for people trying to enjoy each day more. You do not have to be a writer to put this tool to work for you. Get a notebook and begin to jot down thoughts, list priorities, and consider changes you need to make. You might write about your ideal work week, how it fits with the priorities you have identified and possible changes you need to make. Go back to your list of twenty questions and see what jumps out at you.

A few minutes every now and then to take your "job pulse" will help. Everyone has rough days, and most people wonder from time to time if they are in the right spot. But remember that we are to live life to the full—and this means avoiding the Daily Grind Syndrome. You can figure out the highest and best use of your time and what you need to say no to.

Finding Satisfaction on the Job

In Ecclesiastes 3:12-13, we are told of the importance of finding satisfaction in our work: "I know that there is nothing better for men than to be happy and do good while they live. That everyone may eat and drink, and find satisfaction in all his toil—this is the gift of God." When I consider that satisfying labor is a gift from God, it makes me hungry to do such work consistently. You might want to write about this passage in your journal or pray about it, considering what satisfies you on the job and what leaves you feeling restless.

Overcoming Conflicts Between Home and Work

One of the biggest areas of conflict comes between needs at home and needs at work. This takes much prayer and thought—and sometimes it means turning down a career opportunity or missing a family activity.

"Being the best mother I could be is one of the things I want to be remembered for, so that is always a priority," said a woman who is quite good at her job. "Of course, there are times when I have to choose where I am needed most, but *always* my children know that they are the priority. The important thing is that if I have to miss something of theirs for work, I explain to them why. The other benefit of this is that they get an understanding of the importance of taking care of your responsibilities, which hopefully will build in them a good work ethic."

A businessman sets the same priorities: "My career and church involvement cannot be at the price of my family. Can I look back in life and say I was successful or a good church leader but a terrible father who was never there? I cannot."

What is slowing you down and keeping you from being more effective in blending work and home? What keeps you feeling as though you are juggling and have way too many balls in the air?

A Maryland attorney, married with a young son, travels often and has made hard career decisions to keep her priorities in order. "I have been very fortunate to have a flexible part-time work schedule and to work from home. This works for me. I realize that I can't do it all, but I can do this. This didn't come easy, however. I proved to my company that I was a serious, hard, and productive worker before there was a need for any flexibility." Her biggest challenge? "Focus—even more than time. Not thinking about work projects during nonwork time, and focusing on work and not family when I'm working. I constantly need to work on setting limits to protect my family time and my work time."

Whether you finished school recently or decades ago, this is a perfect time to step back and consider what you thought your life might become, what it has become, and what God wants you to change. Most of us have lectured our children or have been lectured ourselves about not yielding to peer pressure. We have to be willing to take that lesson to heart when it comes to living according to our priorities—where we often feel the pressures of others, from family members to bosses to friends and colleagues.

Dust off your priorities and expose them to the light of day. See if they are in order. Update them as needed. Live by them. You will find more joy in your life as you do so.

A PRAYER FOR YOUR JOURNEY

Dear God, help me set my priorities and make decisions accordingly. Show me how to balance and blend the many parts of my life, always loving and serving you. In the name of Jesus. Amen.

Tips from Busy People

Whatever your choices, make sure your actions match your words.

"I'd advise people to figure out what is most important to them and come up with some kind of structure to make sure they can keep that commitment. If you say your family is most important, how do you make sure they're first? Do you create time for them regularly? Do you choose them first over other people and activities?"

Find what you like to do.

"Slow down and make time to think, feel, love, and pray. It's just a job! Nobody really cared that I worried and hurried so much. It became a way of life. Trust in God and yourself."

Chapter Three

God's Guidance

Being Led to the Right Place

Encouraging Word: *God has a plan for the work you do.*
Everyday Step: *Consider your talents and how you are using them on the job.*

Do all the good you can, by all the means you can,
in all the ways you can, in all the places you can,
at all the times you can, to all the people you can,
as long as ever you can.

—*attributed to John Wesley*

When I was ten or eleven, I decided to open a preschool in our vacant garage. I swept out spider webs, hung decorations, and made flyers with a clown logo announcing the grand opening of the Happy Day Daycare (pretty catchy name, eh?). My next-door neighbor humored me and let me babysit a child or two for an hour or so, but within a few days my career in child care began to wane. It felt a little less like play and a little too much like *work*.

By the time I got to junior high, I had begun to think of another possible career: FBI agent. At the end of high school, I was working part-time as a bookkeeper in an insurance agency, with a tempting offer to forgo college and work full time. I chose college and plunged into my journalism career, working to pay my way.

Perhaps you too had several careers in mind—or maybe you are one of those rare people who knew from childhood what you would do. The careers I eventually chose scarcely entered my mind as a child—and yet in some ways, it seems as though everything I ever did came together to shape me for the right jobs. With the perspective of distance, I see God's hand directing and helping me use the gifts I was born with. I know, beyond a shadow of a doubt, that whatever I am doing, I am to let others see Christ through me.

Depending upon God's help in shaping our work choices is crucial. Sometimes these choices are clear. At other times, they take extra prayer and discernment, listening, and seeking the wise counsel of others. For many, money is part of a career choice. Our relationship with money and work requires immense prayer and attention.

Many people have happy stories of God's guidance in their work. At the time I wrote this chapter, my office adjoined a flower shop. I wandered next door to chat (no, I was not procrastinating—well, maybe only a tiny bit). "Does God speak to us about work?" I wondered aloud, directing my question to the owner of the shop.

The business owner did not hesitate in her response: "God leads us to the place we're supposed to be—if we listen."

She told a story of asking God many years ago to help her find a job where she would be happy. She had three small children and wanted work she would enjoy. Soon after that prayer, a friend of a neighbor's asked her to help out in a floral business. "I told her I didn't know anything about that, and she said she'd teach me." She has now spent more than thirty years as the very successful owner of a flower and gift shop, work she has found wonderfully rewarding.

"It just worked out," she said, acknowledging once again God's guidance.

It just worked out.

This is the story many people tell about finding the place they needed to be. When they asked God to help them and listened for answers, remarkable things turned up or a peace surrounded them.

For some, a word from God comes in a surprising way, as it did for a banker satisfied with her career—until she was asked to write what she would like said about her at age eighty. "It was at that point that I realized that the career I was dedicating so much time to was not what I wanted my friends to remember me by." She left that job and became a full-time employee of a church. "I absolutely felt like God was calling me to do this. It was a place of learning for me that God's call doesn't mean you need to preach! It meant changing the direction of my life from one of a career going up the corporate ladder to using the gifts that God had given me in a totally different direction."

"Utilize My Best Strengths"

A friend of mine from college is a school counselor, and she is branching out into a private practice, having always sought the place "where I could utilize my best strengths" and trusting God to help. She says, "I just believe that it is all going to work out because I feel that I am doing what God would have me do. I have worried about the financial aspect and my lack of business knowledge, but I am learning as I go. I am joyous about working with people I like and respect in a positive environment, as well as the opportunity to do good work, helping adults and children."

In serving others, she finds her own daily joy.

Consider the impact you can have on the world when you learn contentment on the job. No matter what work you do, you can make a difference in the lives of people around you. This means recognizing God's place in our workplace, in the jobs we choose and the jobs we keep.

Sometimes it is all too easy to ignore God during work. We are busy, distracted, competitive. We want or need to make more money. We like being in control. Perhaps we even have a tiny sense that we can handle this better if we do not involve God.

That never works out well.

As a woman in my small group said about her job, "If I just run it by myself, it never works out like I want. So I give it to God and follow him."

So why is it so easy to lose sight of God in the daily fray? How can we keep God's plan for us in mind as we make work decisions?

Using Special Gifts at Work

Asking God to help is one of the first ways to involve God in your workday life.

Consider how you were created and the special gifts you have. How might God want you to use those? Do not doubt that God has a plan for you—and that includes the work you do. We can be used in a thousand ways in our everyday roles, whatever and wherever those are.

Perhaps you are wondering if you are in the right place or if God has another plan for you. Consider your talents and gifts and whether your work makes use of these in a meaningful way. "Learn what talents you have and pursue excellence in those," one businessman said. "Don't settle for what you can get by with."

The owner of a relatively new business emphasized the importance of self-knowledge. "Analyze *you*!" he said.

"Everything I read told me to determine what I like to do. What am I good at—really good at? Again, I asked others. I asked those who knew me well, former bosses and employees. I asked others who owned small businesses. You need to have enough money to fund what you do, and you need to have a plan."

You can learn a lot by thinking about your work style and the way in which you work best. Remember, you are "the apple of his eye" (Zechariah 2:8), and God has given you abundant talent. "There are different kinds of gifts, but the same Spirit. There are different kinds of service, but the same Lord. There are different kinds of working, but the same God works all of them in all men" (1 Corinthians 12:4-6).

Consider these questions and how they intersect with the work you do now:

- Are you using gifts you know you have?
- Do you prefer working alone or in teams?
- Do you thrive on challenges and deadlines or do you resist them?
- Do you like influencing others or do you prefer to avoid personal contact?
- Would you rather lead or stay in the background?
- Do you like being creative or do you prefer precise directions and tasks to complete?
- How do you respond to conflict?
- Does your work energize you or drain you?

This list can help confirm whether you are in the right place. If you are dissatisfied with work or you are unsure, this handful of questions can be a tool to figure out what needs to change. While we may not have a perfect day every day, we should have more good days at work than lousy ones. Even on the tough days, we need to believe that we are in the right place for the right reasons. If you consistently find that not to be the case, you might want to take another look and pray about it.

This does not mean that work will not sometimes seem like, well, *work,* but it means that you can enjoy work more. This will be an ongoing balancing act. As one friend told me, "I hear all the time, 'Do something you love, and you'll never have to work,' but I've found that work is work. That said, I've never minded being at the office. I have at times minded not being someplace else."

That "not being someplace else" is an issue that plagues many, and we need to use a variety of skills to deal with the many demands on us. Part of this is learning to listen for God's guidance in how to use our time.

Our lives and, thus, our work are the way God shows up in today's world. We house God's Spirit and are called to share that with the world.

"And in him you too are being built together to become a dwelling in which God lives by his Spirit" (Ephesians 2:22).

Recall why you do the work you do, and pray about whether that is where God wants to use you.

My dear friend, a speech pathologist, is a great example of how such awareness can work. She says, "I was hired straight out of college and have worked in my field for almost thirty years. I have regretted my choice very few times." She says her work pays reasonably well and that it is filled with interesting people and variety.

Beyond that, she says, "In a spiritual sense, it's my ministry. I realized many years ago that I might not be able to fix all of my patients, but I could love them. God calls us to love one another, and this is a daily opportunity for that."

An oncology nurse recently moved into an administrative job. "As an oncology nurse dealing with death and dying, I have always felt that I was called to this area of nursing—one of my spiritual gifts, perhaps. Sometimes the stress of death and illness takes its toll, so you kind of have to back up and take a deep breath and give thanks for what God has given you. When I changed jobs, it was because I had burnout from working too many long hours, and we had an unusually high number of deaths of folks we had cared for for a long time. I prayed for a change, and this computer job opened up, and I thought and prayed some more, and then I took it. I do miss my patients, so burnout may not be a permanent thing, just something to step back from for a while and regroup. I have been praying for guidance in this matter."

Making Work Meaningful

I have always wanted to do meaningful work. I liked the notion so much that the tagline for my business is "Strategies for Meaningful Life & Work." "I'm intrigued by the idea of meaningful work," an executive said. "I can't tell you how often people tell me they admire what we do, and they mention the word *meaningful,* and I'm thinking, what they do is so meaningful! What would we do without janitors, architects, receptionists, engineers, plumbers—you get the picture. I believe that as long as one is doing something legal, ethical, and moral, the work can be meaningful, and perhaps the person doing it can 'minister' to those they come in contact with."

An attorney made a similar point. "All work has value. Don't wait for the perfect job when you need to support yourself and your family. Take the job you have and do your best in it. Always have a personal growth plan and look for ways to improve and to find better work. Be willing to 'do windows.' "

Their points are well-taken—and thought-provoking. Use your gifts each day, and do everything for God.

The Pull of Money

While serving God may be why we want to work, many people choose to work because of money, which can be one of the toughest and most volatile topics to discuss. Sometimes people take a job they do not like because they need to make more money. I encounter many people who stay in jobs where they are unhappy because of the security of their salary and benefits. At other times, people give up great jobs knowing they will have to learn to live with less.

I have been blessed with jobs that paid very well—and I have stepped out in faith to do much less lucrative work. I know some of the hassles of daily life can be eased with a certain amount of money, but true joy does not come from an extra-large paycheck. Still, money concerns are hard to overcome. With most, it seems that whether you have a lot of money or a little, money is still an issue.

"I believe that we should do what we love, and the money will follow," said the lawyer previously mentioned. "Money has never been my 'hot button.' However, later in life, I realized that putting money in perspective, which includes being paid reasonable fees for valuable services, helped me focus on appropriate priorities."

The Bible talks quite a lot about money as it pertains to priorities and the lifestyle we choose. The message is clear that money in and of itself is not bad, but the love of money can be damaging. Is money leading us to certain jobs or is it God's calling? *That's* usually a hard question!

Most of us have daily needs that require a certain amount of money. We want to provide for our families. We also want to be generous with others, such as churches and community charities. That requires money. However, working only for money throughout life is not the best way to enjoy each day more. Being open to God's calling is crucial, in whatever we do and however much we make. Sometimes we may be asked to walk away from a big salary for an even bigger purpose.

The Love of Jesus, Through It All

One of the most chilling stories in the Bible addresses this, in the account of the rich young man who came to Jesus for instruction but did not want to give up his lifestyle. "As Jesus started on his way, a man ran up to him and fell on his knees before him. 'Good teacher,' he asked, 'what must I do to inherit eternal life?' " (Mark 10:17). Jesus walked the man through the Ten Commandments, and the man declared he had kept these since childhood.

> Jesus looked at him and loved him. "One thing you lack," he said. "Go, sell everything you have and give to the poor, and you will have treasure in heaven. Then come, follow me."
>
> At this the man's face fell. He went away sad, because he had great wealth.
>
> Jesus looked around and said to his disciples, "How hard it is for the rich to enter the kingdom of God!"
>
> The disciples were amazed at his words. But Jesus said again, "Children, how hard it is to enter the kingdom of God! It is easier for a camel to go through the eye of a needle than for a rich man to enter the kingdom of God."
>
> The disciples were even more amazed, and said to each other, "Who then can be saved?"
>
> Jesus looked at them and said, "With man this is impossible, but not with God; all things are possible with God." (Mark 10:21-27)

When direct-deposit paydays thrilled me, this story caused me guilt—until I considered it more carefully. How wonderful that Jesus looked at the man "and loved him." How awesome that Jesus gave the rich man a choice. This guy—I picture him nowadays in a crisp button-down shirt with khakis and a laptop computer—was not a bad man. He tried to keep the commandments, and he clearly wanted to hear from Jesus. He simply did not put his priorities in order.

Jesus went on to tell his disciples that with God all things are possible. Jesus did not care how much money the guy had—he cared about the man's relationship with that money. In times when we are greedy and grabby, we can let our true calling slip away. In Luke 12, there is a story about what the Bible calls a rich fool—a story that tells us to be on guard against "all kinds of greed." Many people, including myself, wrestle with this issue regularly: "A man's life does not consist in the abundance of his possessions" (Luke 12:15).

Matthew 6:32 helps put all of this talk about money in context: Our heavenly Father knows we need certain things. A generous, loving God who treats us as precious children does not want us to be hungry, naked, or generally impoverished. God provides.

When Money Contributes to Worry

After this money passage comes a lesson from Jesus about worrying. That is surely no coincidence. For an incredible number of people, money worries push them along each day, sometimes leading to poor decisions.

When we let the love of money, rather than the voice of God, guide our work, we are likely to stumble. My friend and CPA sees this in her work: "The pursuit of money will never satisfy you." She believes the Bible is clear that it is OK for people to be wealthy—but "not if you are doing it for the money, instead of serving others. If you want happiness in work, choose something where you will be serving others. If you choose work because of the money you are going to make, you're probably not going to be happy."

She has given me one of my favorite phrases lately: "the freedom of underspending." One reason people get tied to the wrong job is they overspend, including hanging around big spenders. Often people choose long, hard days at work because they do not want to give up money. An awareness of this choice can help ease stress or lead to a change.

A woman who did shift work at a large manufacturing plant found she had to give up overtime, even though the money was attractive. "I finally came to realize that money ain't everything. Sure, the pay was good, but I found myself thinking material possessions would replace what was missing in my relationships at home. This was a very grave mistake on my part. I quit working the overtime in lieu of spending time with my family."

Do Your Best . . . and Trust the Lord

A former nurse practitioner and attorney pointed me to a great passage in the book of Colossians: "Whatever you do, work at it with all your heart, as working for the Lord, not for men, since you know that you will receive an inheritance from the Lord as a reward. It is the Lord Christ you are serving" (Colossians 3:23-24).

"What I do isn't nearly as important as how I go about it," this woman said. "That doesn't mean there won't be frustrating office politics or discouragement over a deserved raise or promotion that goes to someone else, but it does give a framework for how to handle it: do your very best and trust the Lord."

Wherever we are, God wants us to serve. Some ways are obvious—but not always easy. They include living by principles of integrity, loving-kindness, fairness. Watch what you say and how you say it. Through your faith and the way you act, you can bring God into your workplace.

Just ask this administrative assistant at a large newspaper: "I believe that my workplace is my mission field. That people are brought into my path for a specific purpose for them and for me. The Lord has called me to pray, and I believe it is because he knows I really will. I believe that my most important function is to pray for the directors, the officers at corporate headquarters, and all of the employees who are affected by the decisions being made. So the most important part of my job is done *before* I even come into the building."

Having worked with this woman for many years, I know her to be a committed prayer warrior and many times have asked her to pray for me. People such as this use their gifts in amazing ways to do the will of God.

A great adventure story in the Bible tells about the specific work God had for one man to do—a call to Jonah to "go to the great city of Nineveh and preach. . . . But Jonah ran away from the LORD" (Jonah 1:1-3) and headed to another town. He did not want the people of Nineveh to be saved. His disobedience took a nasty turn, because Jonah was caught up in a fierce storm at sea and swallowed by a whale. Time and again, he received God's mercy. Jonah knew he was wrong and "prayed to the Lord" (Jonah 2:1). Perhaps God will not use such drastic methods to get your attention—but we never know how God will direct us, and we had better be at the ready.

Pray for courage to do what you are created to do and for God's presence in your daily work life. Ask for wisdom as you go in to work. The book of James contains valuable business advice: "If any of you lacks wisdom, he should ask God, who gives generously to all without finding fault, and it will be given to him" (James 1:5). God gives us abundant wisdom if we ask and believe. This is available to us, a free gift of God and a great tool.

At the end of the day, give thanks for the work you are uniquely called to do.

A PRAYER FOR YOUR JOURNEY

Dear God, please give me wisdom to choose the right work and to do it to your glory. Help me serve wherever I am and whatever I am doing. Show me your way for my daily life. In Christ's holy name. Amen.

Tips from Busy People

Love one another.

"Jesus is love. People are important in life. Not power or money. Money and power are by-products."

Remember why you do what you do.

"Recognizing the nonfinancial reasons I work gave me new reasons to feel fulfilled and then enjoy it all so much more. I have only recently learned that making occasional mistakes won't ruin my credibility, which reduced a lot of unnecessary anxiety and has made work much more enjoyable."

Chapter Four

The Freedom of Focus

Organization Brings Its Own Magic

Encouraging Word: *Do not try to tackle everything at once.*
Everyday Step: *Remind yourself each morning of your priorities.*

Many things which cannot be overcome when they are together yield themselves up when taken little by little.
—Plutarch

As a child playing church-league softball, I learned an important lesson the hard way: take your eye off the ball for a split second, and there is a good chance you will strike out or get hit in the head.

That same lesson plays out as we try to hurry less and worry less at work. Once we identify a better approach to work as a priority, we must *focus* on making it happen. In the midst of meetings and deadlines and major projects and daily scheduling, we may be tempted to take our eye off the ball or even to wander around the field, proud that we managed to show up for the game. We often do not allow ourselves to hope for a home run or a victory.

This much-needed focus requires paying attention, reminding ourselves each day of our priorities and staying in the game even when we mess up.

Many distractions demand our attention and can keep us from staying focused. Some of these are put upon us by others—a boss, a coworker, a customer. Others we hammer ourselves with, sometimes through overscheduling, disorganization, and procrastination. These three very ordinary villains become serial killers in our daily lives—killing our enjoyment of work and sometimes even relationships, our productivity, and our overall outlook on how things are going. While they are so fundamental, they keep people from moving on to bigger ideas and issues.

Every now and then my schedule jumps up and hits me in the face, just like a ground ball that takes a last-second hop. You may have experienced the very same thing—when you think you are doing a good job with life and work and, wham, you look at your calendar and panic. Keeping this under control requires being aware that God has a plan for us and that plan is never to live hassled and frazzled. Stop from your busy schedule and consider the words of Psalm 31:14-15: "But I trust in you, O LORD; / I say, 'You are my God. / My times are in your hands.' " When I take a moment to commit my time to God, trusting in the Lord's guidance, I am calmer and get more done.

Pay attention to your schedule—every single day. Try to prevent overloading, and learn how to handle it if it occurs. Do not add this activity and that, thinking it will not matter. This is similar to adding weights at the gym. Five pounds might not seem like much, until you add five more and five more.

Notice what you are planning. Each activity or commitment, even if small, takes time and energy.

This is definitely one of the hardest things for most people to handle, but some people have come up with solutions that work for them, at least most of the time.

When her children were younger, one accountant said no to extras that did not involve her family and friends. "Now it is mostly, if I don't want to do it, I probably should not. If my plate is already full, what goes off if something else comes on?" When she is asked to be a volunteer, she asks how much time is required, and then multiplies that by three. "If I feel called to do it or if it is something I have always wanted to do, I try to figure out how to do it," she says.

A business owner in Texas, who is very civically active, admitted, "I've slept too little and worked too hard." However, he puts a priority on community service and has learned to say no when needed: "I have a personal mission statement which helps me evaluate."

A young professional describes it in a similar way: "We have all been there, looking at the calendar, thinking, *Something has to give*. I ask myself, *If I do this next thing on my schedule, what are the benefits, and who pays the price?* I cannot spend my whole life making others happy and making myself crazy at the same time. Prioritize, pray, and be led to what you can and cannot do."

Important advice: Pray about your schedule and what you say yes to.

Consider your vision for life and how God is prompting you. Make your own guidelines for what you say yes to, taking a cue from the busy people mentioned above. Take a moment to write those down and reexamine them regularly.

Some assignments are mandatory, but others are open for negotiation. Some are personal but affect how you feel at work. If you are overextended, either at home or at work, you tend to be exhausted. That leads to a shorter fuse and less patience with colleagues and clients. Your thinking may be cloudier or you may get what a counselor I know calls "the stupids."

You may very well enjoy lots of activities and commitments and feel as though they help your career or are your responsibility. However, if you try to do everything, you likely cheat those you are best at.

Make sure your schedule lines up with your goals as much as possible.

The creative owner of a public relations firm said she realized that her family must come first and that she needed renewal time for herself and time with friends. This helps her shape her work and volunteer activities. "My problem in saying 'no' was so many things sounded fun and interesting to me. I wanted to do too much. I finally realized I was exhausting myself and had to prioritize, and now I do. I don't look at it as turning something down, I look at it as honoring my commitment to myself."

Wiggle Room

Do not rush into obligations, even appealing ones. I've learned to sleep on answers to some requests to keep from piling on too many activities. Leave gaps on your calendar to be filled in later. If you schedule every moment for a month with a breakfast meeting here, lunches there, evening meetings, and so on, you will be worn out. Leave some wiggle room.

Once more, go back and see if you need to disengage from any commitments. If the thought of your calendar makes you queasy, walk away from something. Balance activities to keep a good perspective. In the busiest season of your work, for example, do not take on a new church class to teach. But in a slower time at work, consider volunteering somewhere.

Organization Is a Wonderful Thing

Even if your schedule is not overloaded, you can feel too hurried when you are disorganized. This feeling engulfs me from time to time. For decades I had my own system of staying organized. The stacks of stuff on my desk could be piled high—as long as I knew what was in each stack. The moment I lost track and started frantically digging through one pile after another, I knew it was time to sort ruthlessly. That method no longer works.

The amount of clutter that accumulates in my office and in my life is like kudzu, that insidious southern vine that creeps along, covering whatever is in its path. I turn my back, and clutter threatens to choke me. Once it was just paper. Now it includes virtual untidiness. I must remind myself incessantly to keep less, toss more.

Disorganization and clutter cause confusion—and they set you up for problems. The exciting story in the book of Judges tells about Gideon's army defeating a much mightier army because the others were disorderly and confused. "When the three hundred trumpets sounded, the LORD caused the men throughout the [Midianite] camp to turn on each other" (Judges 7:22).

This story makes me a bit sheepish because my overly hurried days are days of confusion. One step to winning the battle of too much to do is to be more organized in your approach.

Restoring Order

Set aside time regularly to restore order to your work—to clear your desk, clean out files, and sort e-mails. This is one of those "shoulds" where we often lose focus, but keep at it until you have a system that works for you. This will make a world of difference in your effectiveness at work, saving time and easing stress.

Start with your desk. Those stacks cause your blood pressure to soar as you try unsuccessfully to put your hands on a crucial piece of paper lost in a pile of receipts, notes, and professional journals. Block out time to do a clean sweep of your desk. Sort through, tossing with delight. This might take an hour or two, or an entire day, but it will be time well spent. Even though I urge people not to work on their days off, do so if you must to make this happen. You will breathe easier.

Sort through your e-mail. Get rid of those e-newsletters you have been meaning to read for a month, the "hmmm, good idea" e-mails you wanted to think about. Put important, saved e-mails in folders where you can find them if needed. Empty your "Old" and "Sent" boxes.

Try not to let your inbox fill up again. For years I have been diligent about this, and it helped me focus. While on deadline for this book, I let my inbox grow . . . and grow . . . and grow. I looked up one day and had about 300 e-mails sitting there, staring me in the face. It weighed on me so much that I spent an entire afternoon clearing out, filing what needed filing, deleting what needed to go. When I confessed this, several people said they routinely keep several hundred messages in their inbox.

Sometimes this daily battle of staying organized and calm seems to be gargantuan—but it can be won with small attacks on ordinary enemies such as accumulating e-mails. Remember: little David beat giant Goliath. Surely you can whip some clutter.

Clean out your paper files, too, starting with those you use most often. Keep them neat and useful, not bulging and scary. Move on to the file drawers you have not touched in months or possibly years. Toss. Shred. Smile at the relief you feel. Look around your office, at home or at your place of business, and take stock of what needs to go. Many things once useful now gather dust. For example, in my office, notebooks tend to stack up. Who needs two dozen three-ring binders with ten sheets of paper from a meeting or conference four years ago?

Look at your work space with a critical eye. Sometimes I will visit an office and be amazed at the dusty junk stacked around. It clearly has been there so long the occupant no longer sees it. Recently I took a photograph of my office and noticed a stack of stuff in a corner I had completely overlooked. The picture clearly showed how messy it looked. An outside eye can help too. A friend occasionally helps me tackle my office. Her total disdain for the piles of things I thought were important puts my clutter into perspective and helps me toss liberally—with only a little whining.

Keeping your work area neat can make a big difference in your attitude about work. While most people crave being organized, they often do not act upon that desire because they are overwhelmed. The papers are too messy. The files are too jumbled.

You Do Not Have to Tackle It All at Once

Jot down three things you can do to organize your daily life. Do them. That will give you the momentum to handle a few more. Even small victories give you more energy.

While you are at it, take a look at mental clutter—nagging problems you need to take care of, projects you keep putting off, and useless worries that bog you down.

Grab a piece of paper or your journal and list what these are—those issues that make you feel as though someone is sitting on your head.

Eliminating nagging problems is an excellent way to enjoy each day more. Often people are weighed down by ongoing problems that can be solved in a relatively short amount of time. These range from never having paper in the fax machine to a computer problem that needs fixing. Sometimes solutions are as simple as leaving for work ten minutes earlier, so you can arrive calm instead of frazzled. Perhaps you are very organized at work but mightily disorganized at home. Disorganization at home spills over into our attitude about work. When we worry about misplaced bills or get a phone call about a permission slip for a child's field trip, we lose focus at work. The day becomes more stressful.

Once you have identified these problems—and this probably will not be hard to do—come up with steps to solve them. Recognize them as the deterrents they are to living the life you long for. They are wicked if they keep you from living fully and enjoying each day as a child of God. The Bible has a word about that too: "Do not be overcome by evil, but overcome evil with good" (Romans 12:21). One step at a time, you can win this battle.

Putting Off 'Til Tomorrow . . .

When I ask clients about nagging problems in life and at work, procrastination, the evil twin of disorganization, is often near the top of the list. Many people have made an art out of putting off until tomorrow what they do not want to do today. Putting things off is enticing. However, procrastinating makes life more complicated and tiring. Chores and challenges do not go away. They simply wind up being done on a tighter deadline. This causes all manner of anxiety, which the Bible clearly says is not useful.

Procrastination springs from a variety of places. Maybe you feel you do not have time to do something, so you put it off. But rarely is there more time waiting in the future. Or perhaps you are not quite sure how to do something, so it seems easier to postpone action than to find out how to move forward. Or maybe you choose something that is more interesting or fun—but have a cloud of worry about the undone duty. For too many years I put certain projects off until the last minute. If something urgent popped up, as is often the case in today's business world, I was in trouble. Or I would be scurrying around at the last minute to finish a project, generally angry with myself and everyone in my hemisphere.

Stop to think how procrastination saps your strength and supersizes your stress.

Many participants in my workshops say they wake up in the middle of the night, worrying about what they have put off. Surely restless nights and fretting are not what God would have for us. Remember this verse: "I will lie down and sleep in peace, / for you alone, O LORD, / make me dwell in safety" (Psalm 4:8). Learn to turn off anxious thoughts by praying or remembering a verse of encouraging Scripture. Take care of what is keeping you up at night. If it is a concern about your boss, go to that person. If it is fear about your schedule, consider it calmly and pray for God's help. Talk with your employer or a coworker if needed. Even if it takes a while, devote time to it.

Few problems can be solved in the middle of the night, and we need that time to become refreshed. Sleeping well may be one of the best symptoms of a less hurried and less worried approach to work.

Steps to Stop Procrastinating

Realize God will guide you as you try to get your life and work under control. Make this a spiritual dimension of your life—standing firm in faith, as you sort through this issue of procrastination. "Fear not, for I have redeemed you; / I have summoned you by name; you are mine," says Isaiah 43:1. How encouraging, as we get organized and on track.

- Tackle assignments or projects a bite at a time. Make a timeline, with intermediate steps. Gauge how long each segment of a project takes, and schedule accordingly. Think of this like getting a big meal on the table at the correct time. The turkey does not go into the oven at the same time as the brown-and-serve rolls.
- Using your timeline, do the first step and then the next and then the next. Often a project can be done by grabbing a few moments here and there instead of by blocking off huge amounts of time.
- When you do need a block of time, put it on your calendar, well in advance of the due date. Leave breathing room and you will find that anxiety adjusts accordingly.
- Consider where you tend to procrastinate most. Is it in administrative tasks, such as filing expense reports or keeping client records up-to-date? Or maybe it is in preparing for a meeting or presentation. Dig deeper and figure out why you procrastinate, and how to avoid this.

The author Robert Louis Stevenson said, "Don't judge each day by the harvest you reap but by the seeds you plant."

I like this quotation because it reminds me not to beat myself up if I do not get it all done—but to feel good about getting started and accomplishing what I can.

A PRAYER FOR YOUR JOURNEY

Dear God, thank you for allowing me to cast my concerns upon you and for the promise that you will lift me up. Help me be self-controlled and alert and to keep my schedule under control. Remind me that your mighty hand is at work in my daily life. In the name of Christ, who shows me so well how to live. Amen.

Tips from Busy People

Learn to recognize intense times at work.

"I'm convinced that there is no 'perfect job'—instead, it's up to each individual to manage his time, work schedule, and attitude in order to be a success at work and at home."

Be accountable to others.

"I do much better with maintaining balance if I have an accountability partner, someone with whom I meet to pray, plan, study, and reflect on life and ministry."

Chapter Five

Course Corrections

Staying on the Right Path

Encouraging Word: *You can get back on track, even when you stumble.*
Everyday Step: *Set one work goal.*

God, give me guts. —*Eli Myatt*

A few months back I was headed to meet a friend for breakfast before work. One minute I was driving along normally on an interstate highway. The next minute my car was making an odd noise and was barely drivable. I limped to an exit, ruled out a flat, and slowly started to the repair shop. One of my tires had gotten out of balance, throwing off the entire car—and definitely getting my day off to a stressful start.

This experience is similar to what sometimes occurs in our lives. We are zooming along at seventy miles per hour, with places to go and people to meet. Our to-do list is longer than a child's Christmas wish list. Suddenly, we are completely out of balance.

The answer? Slow down. Take stock. Do what is needed to get aligned again. Try not to panic—and know you can get your life back in control.

After many years of teaching, a schoolteacher told me she still gets excited about going back to school each year. She seemed a bit uncomfortable as she said it, as though she were acknowledging she was some sort of oddball. Maybe you can relate to what she was saying, about enjoying fresh starts and new beginnings, and enjoying your work more when you have a clear perspective.

Fresh starts pop up along our way—the chance to step back and figure out what needs doing differently. Just as the back-to-school season symbolizes new possibilities, unseen adventures, and a chance to do it better, there are many opportunities to start anew with work. I much prefer looking at today and tomorrow rather than yesterday. But it is imperative to look back from time to time—to consider what worked and what did not, and how I can use those experiences.

Seize these openings. Have regular times when you stop to make sure you are on the right path, using any one of several approaches. Reading a book such as this, taking a class at church, or working individually on work-related questions can help.

Set goals and figure out what you want to do.

Some people resist making resolutions, but a written list of goals is very effective. Write down what you want to do in the months ahead.

Unless you know what you want to accomplish, it is tough to make it happen. Goals can help you be nimble and focus on what you want to make happen—and what to walk away from. They can help you decide how to spend time, energy, and money.

Even if you hate the word *goal* and believe in flying by the seat of your pants, some sort of plan can help take care of what is important and anchor you in what God wants. Goals are meant to evolve. You grow from both personal and professional goals. Aim them at achieving the life you were created to live.

An Easy Approach

Quickly list a half-dozen things you want to do professionally and a half-dozen things you want to do personally. Then list things you *don't* want to do in each of those areas. This approach has worked surprisingly well for me for the past few years. It is a super simple way to see what is most important and what is not. Writing it down helps imprint it on your mind. Do not overthink it.

As you take this new look, do it with positive eyes. As it says in Philippians 4:8-9, "Whatever is true, whatever is noble, whatever is right, whatever is pure, whatever is lovely, whatever is admirable—if anything is excellent or praiseworthy—think about such things. Whatever you have learned or received or heard from me, or seen in me—put it into practice. And the God of peace will be with you." The instruction here is to *put into practice* what we are learning and expect God's peace as we do so. Sometimes we see that adjustments are needed, and we know that we have strayed away from the pure and noble approach and are limping into ugly territory.

Another method of regrouping is based on the ebb and flow of activities in your life. Take back-to-school time, for example. This is an excellent time to grade yourself on how well you are doing and to plan for the busy season ahead. This is a time of year when we get back into the groove at home and at work, after the different schedules of summer. There's just something about the cooler air or the change of season and the idea of wrapping up another year that can get your juices flowing.

The Seasonal Springboard

Each year in the fall, I take a close look at where my business has been so far in the year and what needs to happen between then and the end of the year. That provides a logical springboard for planning for next year. This invariably involves both my professional and personal lives—including what I need to give up and what I am considering adding.

You do not have to own a business for this strategy to be effective. This approach can work in any job, at any level.

Fall also presents time to plan for the holidays ahead and to make a commitment to avoid overload at home and at work. For many people, the buzz of overdoing can begin with the start of school, escalate at Thanksgiving, and crescendo with Christmas. Keeping the rhythm of your work in mind during this season eases a lot of worry.

For example, if you are a teacher, you know you will have time off for a Christmas break. You can postpone certain things until then and plan for them. If you are on a church staff or work with a nonprofit organization, Christmas may be your busiest time of year, and you will not want to add extra plans for that season. For people in retail, this is an incredibly hectic season, and it requires immense energy. Go into this time rested, and add as little as you can to your calendar.

Spring, a season of renewal and hope, is another great time for a fresh look at work and for considering a course correction, a time to do spring cleaning of your attitude and to get organized and focused. The observance and celebration of the Lenten and Easter seasons are absolutely wonderful for contemplation and becoming aware. Reflect quietly on God's purpose for your life. "I have stilled and quieted my soul," the writer says in Psalm 131:2. Stepping back in quiet calm is a good way to take stock.

Avoid Hasty Changes

Sometimes you may get restless, but do not be too hasty as you consider course corrections. "Even though I stayed in the same job," a journalist said, "the job didn't stay the same. While change is not my strong suit, it does keep things fresh. As with any job, mine has had its share of highs and lows. There have been several times when I seriously considered either looking for a new job in my current field or moving in a totally new direction. So far, each time I've felt the urge to move on, the circumstances that led to that urge have changed and new opportunity has presented itself. After all these years, I have to think that a higher power has been involved."

When approaching new seasons in your life, consider:

- Am I on the right path? What do I want to do differently? Perhaps this involves your family routine or the way you handle stress at work. Maybe it means setting small goals for a calmer daily life. Maybe it even means doing more. One woman said, "I stress when I am *not* busy. I had one job I was so bored at, I thought it was making me ill."
- How do I move beyond bad times? In workshops and retreats, I sometimes visit with people who are frozen by choices that did not turn out as expected. Therefore, they find it tough to move forward in new seasons of their lives. Maybe the past year has not been that great, or your daily life is overly rushed or negative. What small steps can you take to change that?
- How do I move forward, starting today? This is the day to do things differently. Do not overlook small

changes you can make. Examples: Develop a less-hurried evening or post-work routine to help you catch your breath after a busy day. Do not speed on the way to school or work. Try to avoid using your cell phone in the car.

A colleague gave up her cell phone for Lent, because she wanted to allow more quiet space in her life. Her priest told her it would take discipline, and she found that to be true. The experiment helped her step back and assess: "I think I needed a break. I have been attached to a beeper or cell phone since the early 1990s. I have a personal and work cell phone, and numerous e-mail addresses. I still try not to use the phone in the car on trips, but rather, I listen to self-improvement tapes."

An investment advisor finds that "having the time to think clearly while staying focused" is the biggest challenge he faces as a working husband and father, so he looks for time to step back. "When I am traveling back from a long day out of town and I have a couple of hours in the car alone, that is when I try to download and empty my mind, and get home with a good attitude." This also helps him keep his priorities in order, including knowing that he is doing the work he is supposed to do. "I have come to the realization that when you are frustrated and begin to shop around that the grass is never greener on the other side of the fence. It is still just grass."

Turning to Trusted People

As you consider changes, learn as much as you can, and seek support. Turn to trusted people for guidance, such as a friend, family member, pastor, colleague, or professional counselor.

An outside perspective can be very useful. This works when I turn to others for coaching, and I see it in the lives of clients. One business owner came to see me about the challenge of "the constant balancing act of all my resources, whether it's my time or money, to execute various strategies." She wanted help learning "how to manage myself" and how to spend more time on energizing things, rather than on draining tasks.

She enthusiastically stepped back regularly, began to make use of her journal, and started to see immediate changes. "I'm at a much better place than I've been," she said, a reminder that often it does not take long to see enjoyable changes.

In my business, I have pulled together friends and colleagues to offer suggestions and to help me see if I'm on track. One approach I tried with much enjoyment was having a group of trusted people ask me questions about a business idea. They did not offer answers and only provided their ideas near the end of the day. I found that their questions and follow-up feedback greatly helped me in rearranging components of my work life.

Be open to the unfolding of your work.

"Keep your head and emotions on straight. It's like a roller coaster," one businessman said. "Up and down! Keep moving. Evolving. I've changed every year."

Sometimes our adjustments require us to develop new skills. Through the years, I have worked to learn about each job I was in—or jobs I was interested in. I worked for many years for the same company because I was repeatedly given opportunities to learn and stretch. If you feel stunted, how might you change that? Is there a new area of expertise you can develop?

My brother, a busy insurance agent, has learned Spanish in recent years. This knowledge enhances his personal travel and helps with his business.

A marketing colleague is taking a drawing class, which sparks creativity at work and also is an enjoyable activity for his spare time.

Thirty years after graduating from college, I'm a lot smarter when I realize how much I want and need to learn. As a writer, I find myself hungry for books on improving my craft and eager to attend conferences and courses. As a journalist, I attended many professional meetings where I learned about trends and management.

Have you given any thought to subjects you might want to learn more about—for enjoyment or for usefulness in your personal or professional life? Perhaps it's time to examine areas where you come up lacking and would like to grow.

Learning about any new subject, including other jobs, is fairly simple:

- Narrow the topic. Decide what you want to learn about, and why.
- Head to the library or bookstore to see what books are available to get you going. If you were to count the number of volumes on different topics in my bookcases, you would easily see what I've wanted to learn about in the past—from running a marathon to opening a consulting business to writing books.
- Do online research. One of the startling things about the Internet is the availability of information on the most specialized subjects. We have a flying squirrel nesting in a box in our yard. Wanting to learn more about flying squirrels, we looked online—and found a site dedicated to the subject. Likewise, tons of career information is available.
- Don't be overwhelmed by all the information out there. Take it a bite at a time.

- Mix *learning* with *doing*. Practice what you're learning—whether it is a new language or painting. It is easy to get so caught up in researching a topic that you do not use what you are learning.
- Take a class or attend a conference. Local colleges offer a wide range of continuing-education classes. Can't afford tuition or travel? Listen to educational MP3s or CDs in your car. Also, many local churches provide training options.
- Make a notebook or file, your own personalized resource. Clip articles from newspapers and magazines. Before long, you'll have compiled your own reference guide. I have one, for example, filled with interviews with authors. Every time I come across such a piece in a newspaper or a magazine, I read it, clip it, and save it. That provides inspiration as I move forward in my work as a writer.
- Talk to people who know about the topic you are exploring. People are amazingly generous about answering questions and sharing expertise. Take someone to lunch and pick his or her brain. This is also an excellent approach when you think you may want to change to another field of work. Choose someone you can trust, and learn from him or her.
- Have fun with this. Remember why you wanted to learn in the first place and how this knowledge will enrich your life.

Trial and Error

Begin to pull this together in your life, and know that it takes learning and stepping back for a fresh look—again and again. My sister-in-law, now retired, had a busy career and a family and often had to adjust along the way. "There were lots of false starts," she said. "There was lots of trial and error. I would suggest to people that they not believe they can do it all and maintain it all perfectly. Something, or someone, will suffer. More and more young women are discovering they can take off a few years to rear their children, and then have many years in the workforce. Some have to work out of necessity, as I did, and some are career-oriented. You just do the best you can, try to look out a few years into the future, and make the best decision possible to the benefit of all concerned."

She rearranged her life to focus on priorities: "I did become very enmeshed in my job, which was in public relations at a big hospital. Once, my husband said to me, 'You have no energy left for us.' That pulled me up short. He was right! I began to let go a little at a time of the almost obsessive delight in my work. I knew it wouldn't last forever, but I hoped my family would."

A businessman has learned to know the symptoms of the lack of balance in his life. "I can feel it," he said, and he adjusts accordingly. Some of his signs? Making decisions too hastily, being irritable, and waking up in the middle of the night thinking about work. "That's when Jesus gets called into overtime."

Christ stands by to help us look at new ways with new energy. "Come to me, all you who are weary and burdened, and I will give you rest. Take my yoke upon you and learn from me, for I am gentle and humble in heart, and you will find rest for your souls. For my yoke is easy and my burden is light" (Matthew 11:28-30).

Our untidy, wonderful lives often are filled with trial and error. We feel worn down and want to make sure we are on the right path. Stepping back for a course correction can make a big difference.

A PRAYER FOR YOUR JOURNEY

Dear God, thank you for fresh starts. Help me see what changes I need to make. Go with me as I seek your path for my work. In the name of Jesus. Amen.

Tips from Busy People

Discover what inspires and renews you.

"Name the things that keep you excited about life and work, and make room for some of these. Reading inspiring books, attending motivational events, going on personal retreats, and spending time in the outdoors are some of the things that seem to help."

Exercise for life balance.

"I went home one evening and told my husband I wanted to join a fitness center. I believe with all my heart that God was opening a door for me to feel better about myself and my job, as well as filling a void that was left when our daughter went to college. I had to counter the demands of my job with the demands of my personal life, in which I set up new goals for myself to make me the happiest and healthiest I could be."

Chapter Six

Saying No to Negativity

Choosing a positive attitude

Encouraging Word: *You can make a difference in the world through your relationships at work.*
Everyday Step: *Stop negative thoughts as you notice them.*

Preach the gospel at all times and, if necessary, use words.
—St. Francis

When I turned fifty I went on my first cruise, a fun trip with a group of college buddies. Shortly after boarding the ship, everyone was called to a specific area, where we practiced putting on our life jackets and learned how to deal with an emergency. As I thought of how workmates affect our daily lives, a picture of us all bumping into each other in those gigantic orange life vests popped into my mind.

We jostle each other. We laugh with each other. We even save each other from time to time. No matter how much we like our colleagues, customers, and coworkers, sometimes they, well, get on our nerves. Conflicts arise. Clashes occur. Add to that mix the Really Difficult Person—the "RDP"—who makes it hard to smile and love each day. Some workplaces have one or two RDPs. Some workplaces seem to be overrun with them.

As we seek to serve God and do our daily work with enjoyment, we must learn to work with all sorts of people—those we agree with, those we disagree with, and those we really, *really* disagree with. In my years in business, people have come to me with a plethora of employee problems, ranging from the excellent employee who laughed too much to the coworker who needed a shower to the really smart manager who verbally mowed people down. People problems are plentiful.

A "Successful" Life Is One of Service

Bring on the Golden Rule: "Do to others as you would have them do to you" (Luke 6:31).

That's our directive from the biggest Boss of them all. That means treating *everyone* as we want to be treated, even at work, all day, every day. One person told me this verse shapes her work. "I start from the Golden Rule. My faith tells me that a happy, 'successful' life is one of service. If I am serving others, everything else will fall into place."

Keep this in mind as you consider what you want to say each day to the people around you. Do not blurt out a sarcastic answer or automatically be negative in your approach to another's idea. Remember this same advice when it comes to e-mails. If you are not careful, you might send what a former colleague calls "nastygrams," those hasty e-mails that do lots to tear down and little to build up. Any time you write an impassioned e-mail, give it a little time to percolate before you send it. Consider the tone it will convey.

In all of these daily challenges, only one thing seems to make it all work in a good way: a positive, Christ-centered attitude. Each day we can make a huge difference in the

world by how we treat those with whom we interact. This comes from a great business reference book, the Bible.

Start with the passage containing the Greatest Commandment: " 'Love the Lord your God with all your heart and with all your soul and with all your mind.' This is the first and greatest commandment. And the second is like it: 'Love your neighbor as yourself' " (Matthew 22:37-39).

There it is, laid out for us plain and simple. But those are challenging words to follow at work. They require us to radiate the love of God, which must come from deep within and be ready to spill over into our office, factory, hospital, school, or shop. We must be secure and content within our own skin—loving ourselves. And then we must turn that love right back to everyone we meet—the most difficult customer, the rudest colleague, the harshest boss. Yikes!

We are up to the challenge because we have God's help.

Even in our "other duties as assigned," God is right there to help us love, despite the flaws of others and most decidedly despite our own flaws. Turn to God with the tough issues of attitude and dealing with people. "I tell you the truth, my Father will give you whatever you ask in my name. . . . Ask and you will receive, and your joy will be complete" (John 16:23-24).

Changing Negativity

You likely have worked with people who are hard to be around because they are always negative. This is not unusual because, sadly, we live in a world that tends to expect the worst. For some reason—despite abundance that many people can only dream of—we grumble—at work, in our organizations and churches, even with friends and family.

We wait for the other shoe to drop.

We complain.

We worry.

Most people don't *want* to live with a negative outlook at work, but they slide into it. The older I get, the more I realize how my thoughts shape my day. And *I* can shape my thoughts. Being a positive person is not that difficult, but it does take awareness.

To look on the bright side, shift gears when needed, and trust that things will work out. Remind yourself to stop negative thoughts. Do what you can to improve a negative situation.

"When I find that stress is causing me to think too negatively, I have to work pretty hard at counting my blessings," said a friend who works in middle management for a large business. "It's so much easier to dwell on problems, though!"

Suggestions to remember as you try to get rid of negativity:

- Expect good things to happen. Negative thinking drains energy and keeps you from doing your best.
- Believe in yourself—at work or in an organization or as you try a new challenge. Make a list of your talents and abilities.
- Remember past victories to help you expect future successes. So many times, we do not celebrate accomplishments and positive things in our lives, and we focus instead on failures.
- Don't let past problems or failures at work bog you down. Everyone has experienced some type of sadness or sorrow or tragedy. But we live through those and can come out stronger.

- If you need professional help, such as psychological counseling, make an appointment. The objective view of an outside expert can help immensely in reframing thoughts.
- Don't lose hope. When things are stressful, consider the good in your life and try to focus on that. At the end of a hard day, make a list of blessings.
- Watch what you say, both your tone and your words. "Negative-speak" is easy to fall into—whining and being drawn into gossip or criticizing others. Speak positively.
- Avoid negative people who sap you and harm your outlook. If you work with someone who frequently complains, stay away from that person if possible. Change the subject if you're caught in a conversation, or put a new perspective on a topic. As one worker told me, "I stayed away from all the doomsayers at work who want everyone in the same boat with them. Stay away from negativity and people who tell you that 'you can't.' "
- Remember that your words and attitude have a huge impact on those around you. Be encouraging, not draining. Be the person colleagues seek, not the one they avoid.
- Rely on facts, not feelings, when you begin to expect the worst. If changes are coming at work, for example, ask for information on how these affect you. If you're thinking negatively about finances, sit down and figure out how much you have coming in and how much you have going out. Plan from there.
- Build a spiritual life, with time for prayer and reflection.

God Can Make Things Right

Obstacles pop up and tempt us to be negative. As I mentioned in an earlier book, *Goodbye, Murphy's Law: Whatever Can Go Wrong, God Can Make Right,* I am trying to start a movement to get rid of that sort of thinking. Let us believe instead that when things go bad, God can make them right. For most people, work is a gift—one we rarely stop to say "thank you" for.

Most of the people we encounter each day have faced obstacles at some point in their lives. Many are facing problems this very day, yet go on with grit and determination. That means setting goals, staying on the right path, not giving up. Sometimes obstacles are of our own making, the result of poor decisions in our past. Others are the result of an accident or the action of someone else. Either way, they can be tackled with a positive outlook, no matter how daunting. There is no doubt in my mind that each one of us is supposed to help someone over some sort of obstacle—just as we are to count on others to help us when the time comes.

As one woman said of a job assignment she enjoys, "I would never have done it without prodding from someone who saw potential there I couldn't see myself." See potential. Encourage. Watch how that attitude is soaked up like a sponge.

Develop a Listening Ear

"I worked with all kinds of people, mostly very good, decent people who found themselves in trouble occasionally," a retiree told me. "I tried to provide a listening ear. Most of the time that's all they needed. There were broken hearts, sick children, wayward children, work issues, accidents, problem pregnancies, caring for elderly parents, and all kinds of love stories. When they asked for advice, I tried to put myself in their shoes, use common sense tempered by biblical principles, and go from there."

Many of us have immense blessings, despite obstacles we might have faced, are facing, or will face. Often these blessings help us overcome obstacles, if we can focus on what needs doing and how to do it. Staying above the fray is easy when you think about the Big Picture. It is not so easy when it comes to the day-in-and-day-out details of our daily work. Saturate your work in prayer. Pray for wisdom and insight, kindness and patience. Let this be the foundation for doing work you are called to do and for enjoying it along the way.

Offering Solutions

The world is full of people who can identify problems, and the world is hungry for those who can solve problems and make things easier.

Deal with work challenges in a Christ-like way, as a solution-oriented problem solver. Don't complicate things. Look for the good, and try to make positive things happen. You do not have to be the boss or the business owner to do this. Keep your eyes on how your job fits your professional mission and your personal mission. What do you get paid to do? Are you giving it your best? Spend time on the most important parts of your job. Lose the sarcasm, humor at the expense of others, and petty gossip.

> When we put bits into the mouths of horses to make them obey us, we can turn the whole animal. Or take ships as an example. Although they are so large and are driven by strong winds, they are steered by a very small rudder wherever the

> pilot wants to go. Likewise the tongue is a small part of the body, but it makes great boasts. Consider what a great forest is set on fire by a small spark. The tongue also is a fire, a world of evil among the parts of the body (James 3:3-6).

These are straightforward words about something that plagues most workplaces—problems caused by people who say things they should not. Do not be in that group. You will feel better for it. Be quick to appreciate and celebrate those you work with. Tell people "thank you," and salute good work. Let coworkers know you notice their contributions. You can offer that as a gift back to the world.

Imagine if each of us did that in our daily workplace. Our world would change. We would influence others. They might encourage someone else. This could spread around the world, just through the impact of a few everyday people.

Flavoring for the World

Christ laid out the power of this influence in Matthew 5:13-16:

> You are the salt of the earth. But if the salt loses its saltiness, how can it be made salty again? It is no longer good for anything, except to be thrown out and trampled by men.
>
> You are the light of the world. A city on a hill cannot be hidden. Neither do people light a lamp and put it under a bowl. Instead they put it on its stand, and it gives light to everyone in the house. In the same way, let your light shine before men, that they may see your good deeds and praise your Father in heaven.

These are simple issues that point to sophisticated truths. Most of us understand the difference the right amount of salt makes in a dish, and the way a small light can brighten a dark place. We can have that sort of effect in our work.

"My Christian faith is my job," said one businessman. "Before I 'go to war' every day in my job, and I feel like it *is* war, I read my Bible and ask for God's blessing for the day. I couldn't have my career without my faith. It is what makes me strong and gives me the ability to have a moral compass in a world with no direction. Being a light unto the world, through one's career, can be a powerful thing. People need Christian professionals."

"Love Is the Key"

Be kind to others, whether you are the biggest boss or the lowest worker. Wherever you work, people around you need your care. They need someone to listen to their problems or fears. They need prayer. Christ told us to love our enemies and pray for them. Some of these "enemies" we encounter each day in our jobs. Loving them can be quite hard to do, but it will change your attitude about others—and, thus, how you view your own life.

Many people need encouragement or hope—and you can provide this. A woman who works in a large office said she encourages people by helping them see their situation from a different perspective. "It's hard to see things objectively when you're involved. Love is the key to being an encourager. And that's not the emotion of love, but the *agape* kind of love. It is throwing out lifelines to those who are sinking into despair, depression, or loneliness."

The Presence of the Holy Spirit

A speechwriter in the Midwest prays daily for his coworkers and for others throughout the business where he works. "I rely on the presence of the Holy Spirit to guide me during daily routines and to help me during challenging times."

We must search our hearts and not let selfish motives get in the way. As it says in Philippians 2:3-5, "Do nothing out of selfish ambition or vain conceit, but in humility consider others better than yourselves. Each of you should look not only to your own interests, but also to the interests of others. Your attitude should be the same as that of Christ Jesus."

Look for ways to keep that attitude. Often this comes from being balanced yourself, rested and renewed. Says one artist, "It is easy for me today to turn it all over to God—whether at work or home. Nothing is too small or insignificant. I am also more apt to bow my head at my computer today and thank God for something or ask God for something."

The "5 Ws and 1 H" of Communicating at Work

In nearly every office in which I have worked as an employee or a consultant, people have complained about the lack of communication. They do not get the information they need in a timely way, or they feel that their boss is snide or a coworker talks too much. Workplaces everywhere could be changed overnight if people took to heart these words from James 1:19: "Everyone should be quick to listen, slow to speak and slow to become angry." My natural tendency is to be quick to speak and slow to listen, so I have to work on this always.

Take a hard look at your communication skills. Perhaps you need to reassess your tone or motive for making a comment, your sarcasm or out-of-place humor. A quick tool to help with this is the communication version of the Golden Rule. How do you like being communicated with? Use that

as a guide for how you talk to (or e-mail) those with whom you work.

As a journalist for many years, I wrote scads of news stories that focused on the *who, what, when, where, why,* and *how* of a subject. I've discovered that the "5 Ws and 1 H" can help us communicate better with others. Consider these.

Who: Who do you need to have a conversation with? Who needs to know this information? Don't feel compelled to talk with everyone.

What: What information do you need to impart? Give relevant information. Edit yourself. You probably have worked with people who go on and on, offering more details than you need. I love to talk, and I've often been guilty of this.

When: When should you have a conversation or distribute information? Pick appropriate times for conversations. Give people necessary information far enough in advance for planning.

Where: Where should the conversation be held? Or where is the best place for the information to be posted? Remember: criticize in private; praise in public—and this does not only apply to bosses.

Why: Why is this information necessary? Consider your motive for the conversation. We all have known people who impart information to show how smart they are or how they are the ones who made something happen. While this may be ego-enhancing, it does not help move things forward at work.

How: How will you do this: by e-mail or phone or face-to-face? Will it be casual or more official in tone? Choose the best type of communication for the situation.

Always give others the benefit of the doubt. Do not take offense too easily at what others do and say. As my Grandma Brosette used to say, do not be a bear with a sore paw. It is simple to jump to conclusions, assign blame, and accuse someone of undermining us in the workplace. In most cases, errors and problems occur accidentally. Smile and be flexible.

A woman with a stellar career said she has learned the importance of appreciating others. "The times I would like to forget focus around conflicts with coworkers. I can see now that I didn't take enough time in the early years to emphasize how much I appreciated the hard work of two different people. I took them for granted, and they in turn became resentful and showed it in their interactions with me. Eventually I learned to acknowledge frequently all who help me do my job, and the coworker conflicts disappeared."

Beyond communicating with words, we are always given the opportunity to communicate through deeds. "The strongest message you can give to those who have their eye on you is what you do. They know," one manager said. Our entire being—including our daily work—*is* our spiritual life, with traits such as respect, honor, service, and fidelity. "What other kind of life is there than spiritual?"

You can be a unique and crucial part of the place you work, as different as your fingerprint. No one else can fill your spot just the way you can. You can make an important and distinct contribution, one shaped by God. "Above all, love each other deeply, because love covers over a multitude of sins" (1 Peter 4:8).

Perhaps this perspective will shape your enjoyment of your work and the impact you have on those around you. Do what you can today where you are.

A PRAYER FOR YOUR JOURNEY

Dear Heavenly God, how awesome is your love for each of us, and how rich are the opportunities to help others. Please put people on my path who need my help, and make me alert to those needs. Thank you for my many blessings, for so much good each day. In your majestic name. Amen.

Tips from Busy People

Approach difficult people with patience.

"First, I try to give myself a cool-down period before dealing with someone, as I try to put the offense into perspective. 'How bad is this in the long run?' I make sure I talk calmly and slowly and explain my point of view."

Read the Bible.

"Each year I read the entire Bible through. That has now been true for over twenty years. Each year God speaks to me differently and provides new life lessons. The process has changed my appreciation for the Bible and its role in my life."

Chapter Seven

The Busy Seasons

Managing the Toughest Times

Encouraging Word: *You can make it through super-busy periods with grace.*
Everyday Step: *Get a good night's sleep when crazy days arrive.*

Always do right. This will gratify some people and astonish the rest. —Mark Twain

Picture a batting cage where the pitches keep coming faster and faster. At first you swing and swing and swing again, sometimes connecting and sometimes slicing the air. As the baseballs come at you faster and harder, you duck and cover your head.

Life at work can be that way from time to time—but it should not be that way every day.

This lesson hit home for me (and I do *not* mean hit a home run) while working on this book. Here I was compiling information about how to slow down and enjoy work more. I was thrilled with my path and felt called to be writing this book. I perhaps was even patting myself on the back a bit for knowing how to balance home and work.

Suddenly a series of incidents began to be hurled at me, some of them good and some bad. They ranged from a motorcycle accident my husband had in Alaska to an electrical problem that fried our appliances to the sale of another book and the construction of a new office. Thrown into the mix was a five-week summertime visit from our seven-year-old granddaughter, teaching an adult Vacation Bible School class, and a client crisis. These developments threw me off schedule and made me feel as though my life had been dumped into a blender. This forced me to step back and make a new plan for handling my everyday work better and for meeting deadlines. I felt overwhelmed and frustrated. While I had planned and prayed and thought I had my schedule under control, I was caught off guard by situations that seemed unavoidable.

At certain times, despite our best efforts, we find ourselves swamped. These periods need to be approached with intense focus, extreme prayer, and agile planning.

Maybe, like me recently, you have tried to plan and organize and slow down, but you still have an out-of-control feeling. You are torn between running away to join the circus and glumly accepting the chaos. You may even feel a bit as though no one else really understands what you are up against.

Bear Fruit That Lasts

Over and over again, I have turned to a favorite passage in the Gospel of John, words that describe what God expects of me and a reminder of how much God loves me even when I feel out of control. I absolutely cannot do this on my own and am reassured by the promise that God is the vine from which everything springs forth:

> I am the true vine, and my Father is the gardener. He cuts off every branch in me that bears no fruit, while every branch

> that does bear fruit he prunes so that it will be even more fruitful. . . . Remain in me, and I will remain in you. . . . If a man remains in me and I in him, he will bear much fruit; apart from me you can do nothing. . . . This is to my Father's glory, that you bear much fruit, showing yourselves to be my disciples. . . . You did not choose me, but I chose you and appointed you to go and bear fruit—fruit that will last. Then the Father will give you whatever you ask in my name. (John 15:1-2, 4, 5, 8, 16)

This lengthy passage, the first seventeen verses of John 15, is worth spending time with, and it will help us remain close to God. I love the idea of bearing fruit that lasts—that is what I want to do with my work. We are called to do that, each of us. That fruit could be a book you write, I suppose. It might be a person in your workplace whom you encourage during a rough patch. It might be a donation you make to your church from a bonus you receive. The list is endless, and the concept exciting.

The word *abide* replaces the word *remain* in some versions: "Abide in me, and I will abide in you." My pastor says we too often have "AD—Abiding Deficiency." What are the symptoms? We too often "abide in funkiness," not enjoying life.

One reason for this disorder is the Extreme Busy Season.

Perhaps your stress is a seasonal issue, of the type that is evident in the lives of most businesses and organizations. Examples would include the accounting profession, as April 15 tax day approaches; doctors' offices during flu season; major fund-raising campaigns for nonprofit organizations; spring planting season for nurseries; hot summers for air-conditioning service people; and on and on. Or an Extreme Busy Season may result from a situation born of organizational change: a business opening a new site or expanding a current location, a new top leader taking over, corporate downsizing, or other unexpected staff turnover.

Personal matters often complicate our work lives too: going through a divorce, dealing with a parent's serious health problem, or facing trouble with a child.

Asking God for Help

Take a deep breath and ask God for help. As one professional woman said, "Working where I do can be fun and exciting, but it can also be depressing and stressful. Faith in God has helped me appreciate the former and bear the latter. On one particularly difficult occasion, I found myself in a near-panic state. I picked up my Bible and opened it at random, straight to Isaiah 41:10: 'So do not fear, for I am with you; do not be dismayed, for I am your God. I will strengthen you and help you; I will uphold you with my righteous right hand.' Since then, I try to remember that moment and that passage whenever I feel overwhelmed."

Receive Comfort from the Bible

Remember this most precious reminder: "The LORD is my shepherd, I shall not be in want. / He makes me lie down in green pastures, / he leads me beside quiet waters, / he restores my soul" (Psalm 23:1-3). As I read that, I feel a calm I badly need. I realize God will provide. The image of lying down in a green pasture or being led by the hand beside quiet waters begins to restore my soul.

These busy seasons can be trying and tiring, but perhaps you have more room to maneuver than you think. One CPA wrestles with tax season each year and has learned to make it more manageable by taking one day at a time. "I remember that every day is different," she said. "I have learned to turn off the worry tapes. I remind myself that it is a marathon and not a sprint, and that I have done it before, and that it might actually get easier! I quit trying to cook as much, and use every convenience that I can. I ask for more help and understanding from my family. I try to give myself one day a week for resting—no commitments to anything unessential."

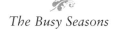

We can find new ways to deal with high-stress, extra-busy times. Look at whatever season is ahead and anticipate scheduling decisions. You know when certain events, commitments, and holidays will fall. Plan around those instead of plowing through them. Certain seasons come with built-in layers of activity and require extra attention. These include back-to-school time in the fall and the Christmas season. The month of May can be a magnet for activities too. You might want to schedule a business trip at a different time when possible or choose a different continuing-education class or limit personal activities.

Tips for the Very Busy Season

- Step back to get a clear picture of how long this stressful time is likely to last. Realizing that this will not last forever is extremely comforting.
- Organize the flow of your project as much as possible by breaking it into bite-sized pieces. Everything does not have to be done in one day. I find it useful to plot out a detailed week or month at a time when things are especially hectic, which helps me keep a steady pace going.

- Avoid unnecessary tasks or projects when you are swamped. The busiest time for your business or organization may not be the time to rearrange the layout of your office or to paint your house.
- Don't sacrifice exercise and sleep. Take a morning walk or continue your weekly tennis game. Give up the nighttime channel surfing, and hit the hay at a reasonable hour.
- Allow yourself small treats or rewards. So you can't take a weekend or even a full day off? Putter around the yard on a Saturday morning, slip away for a round of golf on a beautiful day, or take your family out to dinner.
- Make time for worship. When we get busy, we often nudge church out of the picture. I have found that when I make worship a priority, I get extra energy and encouragement—from God and from the people in my community of faith.
- Plan a fun break to look forward to—a vacation, a few days at home, or a long weekend with someone you enjoy after the busy season passes.
- Keep the situation in perspective. I have had to overcome a tendency to go off the deep end when slammed by my schedule. I reassure myself that I will finish with the frenzy and do better next time. Remind yourself why you are in the situation you are in—often it is because of good choices you wanted to make. Be thankful for the opportunities coming your way.
- Don't beat yourself up. Keep looking for ways to slow down and enjoy each day more, doing the best you can. During certain times, it may be nearly impossible to live as simply or calmly as you wish

in the job you are in. However, this does not have to be your regular, year-round approach to life and work.

- Keep putting one foot ahead of the other—and celebrate your accomplishments as you make it through the most intense times.

One way to deal with these overloaded times of life is to keep deadlines from being brutal. I have a vivid memory as a young newspaper reporter. It was late on election night, and the longtime editor was standing over my shoulder as I wrote a front-page story for the next day's paper. "Let it go," he said, "or I'm hitting the button for you." My lesson on deadlines was cemented in that moment.

Getting things done on time is a big part of enjoying your occupation more.

Many people I encounter are pretty lousy at meeting deadlines. An incredible amount of stress is unleashed because folks wait until the last minute to start on projects.

Take the "Deadly" Out of Deadlines

- Put deadlines on your calendar. Take a look at your calendar every day—not just for that day but for the days and weeks ahead.
- Plot out steps to meet the deadlines, backing up from the deadline with manageable tactics.
- Figure out the information you need to meet a deadline, and begin gathering it. For a mailing to go out for your fund-raiser, for example, you need names and addresses. For taxes, you need records and receipts.

- If you have multiple deadlines at or near the same time, space out the duties and check something off your list. Do not expect to finish all projects at the same time.
- Remember our archenemy, procrastination? Sometimes having a deadline hanging over you is worse than the project itself. Make a start. If you put every action off until the last minute, you increase your tension.
- Build in time for unwanted surprises, such as the flu, a problem at your business, or a family emergency. I have learned this lesson so many times through the years, and even anew while writing this book.
- Don't push your deadline crises off on others. One of the most irritating things you can do to a colleague or fellow volunteer is to expect him or her to clean up your mess at the last minute.
- Meeting deadlines can improve your credibility and let people realize they can count on you. We all know people who never make a deadline, and we sometimes find ourselves not trusting them to come through.
- Set deadlines for yourself to achieve your goals. As bothersome as deadlines are, they make us much more productive. I set deadlines for myself for most major projects and often smaller ones, to be accountable to myself for accomplishing a goal.
- Do not let deadlines cause you to fret. When your stress level accelerates due to a deadline, pause to assess. Consider whether the deadline is important and what will happen if you miss it. If it is critical, make a to-do list and get going. If it is marginal,

decide what truly needs to happen. And if it is unimportant, push it aside and move on.

Resist the Enemy Prowling Through Your Day

Ponder these words from the Bible and how they might speak to your situation: "Humble yourselves, therefore, under God's mighty hand, that he may lift you up in due time. Cast all your anxiety on him because he cares for you. Be self-controlled and alert. Your enemy the devil prowls around like a roaring lion looking for someone to devour. Resist him, standing firm in the faith" (1 Peter 5:6-9).

This dramatic passage helps when I begin to think no one can possibly understand how busy I am or why an activity is important. This is not a very attractive place to be. Perhaps you occasionally find yourself there too. These verses move me forward when it seems as though the spot is too difficult to be fixed.

I must humble myself "under God's mighty hand." God is not all that impressed with how I manage to overload myself but wants me to ask for help in being lifted up "in due time." This overload quandary did not happen overnight, and I will not get out of it overnight. Changing myself requires self-control and alertness. Sometimes we think our lives are hopelessly overloaded, but ultimately it comes down to our own self-control. Piling on is a lack of self-control, plain and simple. I love the word *alertness* in this passage. Stay alert to what you have to do to avoid piling on and putting things off.

Throughout my life as a believer, I have wondered what form the "devil" takes in our lives today. The cute guy in a red suit with horns and a pitchfork is not how evil looks. Instead I see ongoing temptation in overdoing it. That's another reason I like this passage from First Peter so much. Here is my enemy the devil prowling around, looking for ways to derail me from doing what God wants me to do. Taking on too much, I do everything less well. I am less loving and do not enjoy each day to the fullest. I must cast my anxiety on God, who cares for me, be self-controlled and alert, and stand firm in my faith. Those very words cause me to breathe deeply and relax.

The Relief of Forgiveness

In the busy seasons, which are trying and tiring, you may sometimes feel as though you have let God and others down. Here you must pause and ask for forgiveness, for the selfishness or overzealousness or whatever it was that led you to feel out of control. As my pastor regularly reminds us, each time we come into God's presence we can begin again. We can be restored.

When you are overwhelmed, it is essential to stop, if only for a moment, and turn to God for help, knowing the Lord will guide even in something as minor as panic about an overloaded schedule. Allow God to help during these times, giving wisdom and the peace that passes understanding. Make more of an effort to abide in Christ, knowing that *abiding* will help you bear fruit in a way that no labor or overdoing it ever can.

Look at Acts 3:19 for a boost: "Repent, then, and turn to God, so that your sins may be wiped out, that times of refreshing may come from the Lord." Ask God to forgive you for getting so caught up in the whirlwind of work. Know that God forgives you and offers a chance for a fresh start each day.

Welcome the times of refreshing.

A PRAYER FOR YOUR JOURNEY

Dear Creator, help me remember that you are with me in the busiest of times. Show me how to pause and worship. Please deliver me from worry during stressful times and guide me to being effective in how I use my time. Renew me each day. In thy holy name. Amen.

Tips from Busy People

Get plenty of rest regularly.

"The concept of Sabbath rest that can be found in the Bible has become an important ingredient for me to stay in balance and give my best to work, home life, and recreation. Sometimes life's demands can tip this out of balance, but I look for the next early opportunity to take a break and get back in balance."

Make adjustments when the unexpected happens.

"It has not always been so, but I have begun to learn to more readily go to plan B, C, or D or even further down the alphabet when important and unexpected situations develop. Trying to keep the important things in focus when dealing with immediate crises is a challenge for anyone—and it requires great flexibility and often creative thinking."

Chapter Eight

NEW TERRITORY

TRUSTING GOD WITH BIG QUESTIONS

Encouraging Word: *God goes before us as we try different things.*
Everyday Step: *Be open to change.*

Anyone who has never made a mistake has never tried anything new. —Albert Einstein

At times life can feel as though you are standing on a pier with one foot in the boat. You have to decide if you are going to stay put or jump in the boat—and if you don't make the right decision at the right time, you could wind up in the water. You may find yourself at a turning point, desperate to make a decision.

An associate pastor at our church took a new role within the denomination, an opportunity that required relocating. The topic of her touching farewell sermon was "entering new territory," and it reminded me of how God goes before us in each of the work changes we make. She read from Genesis 12:1-4:

> The LORD had said to Abram, "Leave your country, your people and your father's household and go to the land I will show you.

> "I will make you into a great nation and I will bless you;
> I will make your name great,
> and you will be a blessing.
> I will bless those who bless you,
> and whoever curses you I will curse;
> and all peoples on earth
> will be blessed through you."
> So Abram left, as the LORD had told him.

Abram took "all the possessions they had accumulated and the people" and "set out," as it says in verse 5. Along the way they worshiped and trusted God for each next step of the journey. Just the same for us, God reaches out to bless us in ways that are beyond our imagination.

Trust God for each next step, knowing divine help will be there. Ours is a dynamic world, changing along the way. We are to walk faithfully and prayerfully and to be a blessing to others, just as we have been blessed.

Every time I turn around, I come across an individual about to set out for a new place, usually heading straight into uncharted lands. Sometimes these journeys are planned and anticipated. At other times, they happen because of changes in the community, in the economy, with technology, or through a shift in a person's heart and priorities. Some are big relocations, household moves that can be tough on body and furniture. Others are small transitions. Often they involve personal issues that affect every part of life—a marriage, a divorce, an illness, an empty nest, retirement, or taking a buyout.

Always there is that moment of decision when the person decides to jump into the boat or stay put on the pier.

As a writer and consultant, it seems that entering new territory is part of what I do—again and again. This makes life exciting and interesting, and it gives energy and invigorates. However, it is also a challenge that can be frightening at times and requires me to pray consistently, learn constantly, and trust God intensely.

When I began to assess my life and work about a decade ago, I realized God was nudging me in new directions. Plenty of fears floated around in my stomach—what other people would think, the need for money, a concern about seeming reckless or flighty. Ignoring the call did not work. God had left a message in my heart that could not be erased. This eventually led me to leave my secure and challenging work as a newspaper editor and jump into a whole new place. Many times through the years, I have also made smaller changes as the result of prayer and reflection.

At some point in your life, you will likely experience the urge to make a change at work. You may want a new challenge or feel a new calling. You may want to move at a slower pace or feel the need to relocate. Some people work in one place for a long time, sometimes changing roles along the way and entering new territory while staying on familiar turf. Or you may find that you sense changes coming in your industry and want to try something different.

Adapting to Change

The topic of change requires regular attitude adjustments. People continually talk about the challenge of change. In the dozens of newspapers, businesses, churches, and organizations I have visited in recent months, the theme seems to be the same: change is necessary. And it is tough.

Every organization is trying to figure out how to be relevant and useful in a world that is changing so quickly. It is hard to keep up. Most know they must change if they are to grow and thrive. They may not jump in wholeheartedly, but they are wading in, understanding that they must do something. It is fascinating and a bit troubling to watch how reluctant most people are to change, how they cling to the past, and how some think that if they resist change long enough, it will magically go away. Some individuals are stubborn and believe that if they dig in and say no enough, they won't have to change. Others are the hit-and-run changers who make a small effort without following through, quickly going back to their comfort zones. Some resort to either/or thinking, suggesting that all the good traditions will be thrown out for gimmicky new ways. They overlook the blending of old ways and new ways to make life and work better.

"Change is never easy whether it's for the good or not," one employee said. "But I've come to realize that it's one thing we can always count on happening. I deal with change as a matter of survival. If you are not willing to change, you'll become extinct. I would suggest to others to view change as a way to remain young, vibrant, and open to the future."

Most of us have to change unless we want to be endlessly frustrated, lose our jobs, or go out of business. If we don't learn to accept and even enjoy change, we will spend lots of time being miserable.

An established businessman in the West said he has encouraged his children to be intentional in their work and to expect change. "Have a plan or a goal and pursue it. Don't take the path of least resistance. I encourage them to take risks. I think I've given the idea of security too much weight. I also tell them, 'Things change.' It is critical now more than ever to stay on your toes, ready—no, *eager*—to adapt."

Stop for a moment to recall changes in your work in the past few years and changes that are likely to occur. Perhaps you get excited about some, depressed about others. Adapting is hard—but it is important. We sometimes resist change because we do not understand why it is needed or we do not know how to do the new thing asked of us. This is an important time to step back for a fresh look—to consider what we need to learn. When I was a young journalist, newspapers switched to using computers. I recall an embarrassing lesson on learning to use a computer mouse, scooting it here and there, trying to make the cursor do what I wanted, with little success. Now I use my computer all day, many days—and never give the mouse a second thought.

Here it is again: Change happens.

"Knowing when the time is right for a change is difficult," one friend told me. "That is where a lot of prayer comes into play. You also have to have a good sense of where your strengths and weaknesses lie, which will help you make decisions about change and whether a different job may complement those strengths. I really don't dread change. There is excitement in change, at least for me, so I generally embrace something new and different." If you decide to stay in your current job, you may well find yourself facing change. Having taken a buyout from a large company, one woman said, "If they stay, they have to be open to change to succeed, I believe."

Sometimes you are not given a choice about change, such as being laid off or fired. One client says, "I was downsized to reduce expenses. For a pre-Baby Boomer, it is tough. I was raised to be loyal to my employer and work at it like it was my business. I had to take time to get over the shock and start thinking about what to do next. Too many folks jump quickly because they think they must have a job. Invest in yourself for a few weeks. We don't think enough."

During this time of transition, he exercised, read, and observed others. "I let God work on me and the situation," he said. "I asked others what they thought. I got counseling.

I had to get over being mad and the feeling of failure. I had to accept. I prayed! Then, I made a plan." He wound up opening his own successful business.

One way or the other, new territory is often a part of our daily lives, and learning to enjoy this unknown place can make life more enjoyable.

Our attitude about change reveals a great deal about our faith, our trust in God to give us wisdom, and our ability to help others through difficult times. I saw a sign at a church recently that read, "Under same management." Even when our work world is whirling by, God is a rock.

A Map for Changes

In my experience, few things are harder than contemplating a major change at work. The status quo is a pretty cozy place, even if you are dissatisfied with your workplace. Contemplating change brings up all sorts of fears and concerns. Prayer definitely needs to guide you during this process. Listen for God's voice, and do not rush into a change. Know that God will strengthen you on your way and that Christ's love for you is immense:

> I pray that out of his glorious riches he may strengthen you with power through his Spirit in your inner being, so that Christ may dwell in your hearts through faith. And I pray that you, being rooted and established in love, may have power, together with all the saints, to grasp how wide and long and high and deep is the love of Christ, and to know this love that surpasses knowledge—that you may be filled to the measure of all the fullness of God. (Ephesians 3:16-19)

Do not make a change if you are uneasy about it. Sometimes the time is not right. As a Realtor told me, "When in doubt, *don't.*" In other words, wait for clearer direction from God, do more research, and be patient. *Big* changes, in particular, should not be made in haste. While we may not know everything with absolute certainty, often we have a pretty good idea of whether something new is right or not.

This does not mean that all fears or worries must go away. Sometimes we make major changes despite fear. When I left my excellent job to start my business, I was quite scared. But I also knew it was the right thing to do and very much felt God's presence.

The Support of Those You Love

Many factors go into venturing into new territory. One combo is insight and support from people you love and trust. Your spouse or significant other needs to be part of this decision. Making a leap without consulting that person is ill-advised. As a retiree said, "I feel like if my husband supports me in my endeavors, I can accomplish anything!" Another very busy and successful woman relies on similar support: "The only way I am able to juggle this is with the help of a wonderful husband!" Interesting, isn't it, that both women used exclamation marks to emphasize this particular point.

Your decisions affect those you are closest to, and you need to talk with them about financial implications, quality-of-life changes, and the impact on your household.

Whether you are married or single, young or old, finances likely play a part in a change. When clients want to quit their jobs and try something new, I encourage them to gather basic data before they act. This includes a look at how much money they need each month to meet their financial obligations. Sit down and review how much you spend each month and how much you have coming in. If a change means a cut in income, it likely means a cut in expenses. This is one of the hard parts of being a grown-up. To quote one of my husband's favorite movie lines: "It's not the money. It's the stuff."

Consider what you are willing to give up in order to make a change. What are your fixed expenses (house note, car note, and so forth), and what are your optional areas? Where can you save?

Perhaps you are considering a change with—or even because of—a salary increase. A veteran employee is adamant that this should not be the only reason for a job change. "My first rule, now that I am wiser, is never leave a place where you think the boss really likes you. The second rule is stay where you are happy and don't move only for more money. I learned the value of happiness versus money the hard way."

Another topic to look at when considering a move is health care. This particular issue affects many of the people I coach on making big work changes. When I started my business, I was able to get insurance through my husband's job as a schoolteacher. This helped reassure us financially, even though I was taking a big pay cut starting out. Do you have health benefits at your current job, and will you have comparable benefits with a change? Can you get health insurance through your spouse or purchase coverage on the side? Your need for insurance likely depends on your age and health, but most people want to make sure they are covered.

Beware of Daily Fretting

Maybe you are contemplating a change at work, and it hangs over you every day. You wonder, *Is this the day I will quit?* or *What in the world should I do?* Try not to fret about it constantly. You may know, for example, that you want to wait until the end of the school year or reach a certain milestone at work before you make a big change. Set a time to consider your options based on those timelines. Otherwise it will bother you regularly, even if the time is not quite right to make a decision.

When you are ready to decide, pray, and use the tried-and-true "pros and cons" list. You may not be swayed by the actual numbers of positives and negatives, but the list can clarify your thinking.

As you move forward:

- Be informed about the place where you are going—whether it is a career change, the need for more education, or moving to a desk across the room.
- Go toward something you want instead of running away from where you are. Realize that you will give up certain things along the way.
- Anticipate anxiety. Anxiety is a part of transition, so get used to it. A counselor I visited used the term "ANTS" to remind clients that Automatic Negative Thoughts occur during times of transition.
- Allow yourself to be excited. Entering new territory can open possibilities you might never have considered. It can show you things you thought you would never see. It can keep you from getting bored or in a rut. It can even be fun.

A reassuring thing about a change is it does not have to be forever. Sometimes you can get so caught up in trying to plan the rest of your years that you miss opportunities for this part of your life. Most of the time, you can turn around if you must. If you find yourself in a place you don't want or need to be, consider ways to get out.

"You never know where something temporary will lead you and who you might meet along the way," a former colleague said.

Sometimes too you contemplate a change because you know somehow your soul is at stake, either in how your company handles ethical issues, your own integrity, or the demands your career puts upon you. This is particularly hard to deal with in one way and impossibly easy in another. As you decide, think about these words from Matthew 16:26: "What good will it be for a man if he gains the whole world, yet forfeits his soul?"

Stepping Away from the Comfort Zone

Sometimes you just have to get out of your comfort zone—even if it leaves you shaken, rattled, and rolled. We tend to be creatures of habit and to enjoy things in a nice routine—which can easily develop into a rut. By trying new things, going new places, and meeting new people, you learn and grow. Seeing things in new ways can make you more creative at work and help you see how your goals are developing. A change of scenery can also be useful in making decisions down the road.

During one recent year, I went to a retreat center in Kansas, and I met people of a different denomination from mine who were learning about midlife spirituality and retirement. The setting was calm and quiet. Then I went to a publishing meeting in New York, a noisy mass of organized chaos, with booths representing dozens of publishers. That same season my husband and I took an adventurous vacation to South America, a chance to explore and experience winter during the hottest days of summer at home. All of these experiences, in their own ways, helped me stretch and put me into new territory. Those trips helped my perspective and my decision making. Such ventures, even if they are not far from home, can help you decide whether it might be time for you to enter new territory more permanently.

Allow Time for a Change

When you decide to make a major change at work, keep your Big Picture in mind. Often the process of change takes longer than you planned. It took several years of praying and planning for me to make a major career change—and I am not a very patient person.

Others have told me similar stories, such as the medical professional who moved to Seattle after decades as a Texan. "Through these years of working in varied specialty areas within speech pathology," she said, "I realized I enjoyed one area more than the rest. Eventually I set a personal goal of working exclusively in that one area. Due to the nature of the job, I knew it would require a move to a big city. It dawned on me that if I moved to a new area of the country or even overseas, I could meet my goal of specialization, plus the move itself would be somewhat of an adventure."

She took a variety of steps along the way, including a small move within her company. "This move built my confidence in being able to start over again in a new place all by myself, both professionally and socially." Next she focused on continuing-education efforts on her own time to develop in her specialty, and she began to get family responsibilities in order. Three years later she started to look at job postings, and nearly a year after that, she took "the job I dreamed of."

This process can be tough. We are impatient people. We live in an impatient world, and we tend to want changes on our terms, on our timetable.

Tips If You Are Contemplating a Change

A friend who worked at a manufacturing plant for many years described her own wait for the right decision. When buyouts were first offered, the terms were not adequate, but two years later, she thought the time might be right. "I started praying, asking God to help me make my decision." Her words of advice:

- Pray for guidance. This is number one.
- If possible, see how things have worked out for others in your position (those who have left, others who have stayed, and so on).
- Define your requirements. Make a list. Study your finances. Explore possibilities for the future.
- Have faith. You don't have to have a clear picture of where you are going. Let God shine the light ahead, one step at a time. The Lord will get you there.
- Talk to people whose opinions you value—people with experience and knowledge, people you respect, people who will be positive and build you up and be honest with you.
- Stay away from negativity.
- Pray, and pray some more.
- Read books that might be helpful in your decision. "I did a forty-day guided journal that helped me a lot!"

Expect the best in such times of change. Know that God's plan for your life is mighty, that God has equipped you to handle that plan, and you are to follow it. "God's gifts and his call are irrevocable," we are told in Romans 11:29. *Irrevocable*. The Lord is not going to repossess your gifts or lay you off from the special plan for your life.

We grow. We seek. Who knows what adventures God has in store for us in new territory?

A PRAYER FOR YOUR JOURNEY

Dear God, steady and constant in this world of change, help me make needed changes, and remind me that you are with me when I venture into new territory. Sometimes changes seem so uncertain. I ask for wisdom. In Christ's name. Amen.

Tips from Busy People

Avoid impulsive decisions.

"I would encourage anyone to follow their heart, discover their true passion in work, weigh all the factors, including family and finances, pray, seek wise counsel, and go for it."

Do your homework before relocating.

"Be clear on the goals and objectives of your employer. Spend time in the town prior to relocating. Pray, and ask God to lead you to the right decision. Give yourself at least six months to make mistakes, learn your new environment, and so on. Transition is much more difficult than you think it will be."

Chapter Nine

Time, Talents, Money, Mission

Giving something back

Encouraging Word: *Opportunities abound for us to give of ourselves.*
Everyday Step: *Find a cause you are passionate about.*

How wonderful it is that nobody need wait a single moment before starting to improve the world.
—*Anne Frank*

The people who inspire me most are those who manage—no matter how many juggling balls they have in the air—to offer something back to their communities and churches enthusiastically, either through their work or free time. They do that with energy and excellence and a sense of excitement. It seems contradictory, actually—adding something else to their plates. They weave it into their lives as a priority, stepping back as needed at certain seasons.

These people have learned to live large, to enjoy each day and to lead with joy. They combine paid work and volunteer efforts to make the world a better place for all of us. Many serve their churches, both with time and money.

Deciding how you will interact with the community in which you live is important if you are to live abundantly. You will make daily choices about church involvement and other good causes. Some people handle it exceedingly well, knowing what their priorities and passions are and knowing when to step back. Many are energized or refreshed by their efforts for others. However, other people are so worn out at work that they find it nearly impossible to offer themselves elsewhere.

This is a big hurdle to get over as you seek to hurry less and worry less at work. A sure sign I am too busy at work is when I do not feel as though I have time to help with a class at church or to be part of a community function. Being a good steward of time and talent is not up for debate, according to the Bible: "Freely you have received, freely give" (Matthew 10:8). Part of that charge might well be figuring out where you want to serve and beginning to take steps to have time for it.

Take Note of Others

Notice how these involved, active people do it. They have learned ways to be more effective at what they do, to use their gifts, and to say "no," even to great requests. They make decisions consistent with their priorities. Recently, for example, I was at a church meeting with a dynamic volunteer. I wanted him to attend a seminar our church was involved with and might have been . . . ahem . . . *pressuring* him a tad. I admired the way he responded, politely telling me that he had other training opportunities and that he planned to use his time elsewhere.

As I drove home that evening, I realized what a wonderful example he was of not trying to do *everything* but being involved in many good causes all the same.

We are called by God to be good stewards of what we have been given. This means that those who have been given much should look for ways to give back. Opportunities often come to serve the community through our jobs. This may be a one-time volunteer effort, such as raising money in a walkathon or helping repair houses in a poor neighborhood. It may be ongoing civic service, in a leadership role on a committee or within a nonprofit group.

Being an active, committed part of a community helps enrich our lives, while allowing us to show our thanks to God. We can touch lives in positive ways—if we do not overdo it.

"When I was young, I did anything that anyone asked me to do, as I was building my community resumé," one man said. "In my middle age, I now ask myself some questions when I consider community service:

- Is this something I am uniquely qualified or positioned to do at this time? Can someone else do it, or could I do it at a later time?
- What impact will it have on the community at large, and is it worth the commitment and sacrifice?
- Am I considering it because it is worthwhile or because I'm flattered to be asked?
- Is there sufficient support from a capable team that it is likely to succeed?
- Where does this fit in God's plan for my life? Is it something he wants me to do?"

The Fun of Service

This man sees service as his hobby. "I don't hunt, fish, or play golf or tennis. I'd rather be helping on a community project than pursuing a hobby. It's part of my fun. That's not a criticism of hunters, fishermen, or golfers; it's just how I'm made. I can't do things that I do and have those time-consuming hobbies. It's a choice I've made."

The owner of a marketing and public relations firm takes a similar approach: "To me, it's critical to give back," she said. "At first, I did it to get the firm's name out in the community. But for years now, I have realized volunteering was a gratifying way to give back to the community, and it is an honor to be allowed to serve. I've said for years the criterion for choosing where to get involved is to get involved with something you're passionate about. If you don't care, don't bother."

Choosing where you will serve will involve noticing what you care about—the causes that grab your heart or make you want to help.

"I have chosen to put the efforts of my time, outside work, where I feel like I can make the most impact and be spiritually fed the most," said one leader. "My time for my church, although valuable, is immeasurably returned to me by blessings in many forms from God. The time given at church creates a balance in my life so that all is not for me or for selfish indulgences, but for others. Time given is fulfilling."

Another person feels the same way about civic work: "I've gained so much from my community service. It was an 'aha' moment when I realized it was my hobby. I have developed criteria for things I'm willing to participate in, which helps me avoid saying 'yes' too quickly or getting flattered into doing something I don't feel passionately about."

Prioritizing to Support Ministry

One busy investment advisor is usually on the go with his job, with his family of four children adopted from four countries, and with church work. His efforts are clear to him: "I don't really feel torn. It is a matter of prioritizing your activities. I work to support my ministry. That is my bottom line. I am most fulfilled when I am involved in missions work either here in the U.S. or abroad. So I work hard, and I work to be successful to have the financial capabilities to do what I love."

He suggested using priorities to decide what to volunteer for. "If it doesn't feel right, don't let someone twist your arm to be involved. You will not give it your best efforts, and if I can't give it my best, I am not going to be involved. I have been on committees and resigned because the skills they needed, I did not have. I got out of the way and let someone else step in, and they did a marvelous job."

What You Could Be Doing

Even if you are exceptionally good at juggling a mix of options, do not let the importance of sometimes saying no slip away. Depend on a friend, spouse, or colleague to help you.

One executive said he occasionally turns down requests because they cause conflict with his wife, and he knows that he has overloaded. He takes a piece of paper and lists "Things I am doing" and "Things I could possibly be doing." He considers the time it will take to add something and decides if he can do it in a reasonable manner. If he declines a request, he says, "I'm overcommitted, and I cannot agree to do this unless I can give it what it deserves." One office manager uses lists too, "Why to do it" and "Why not to do it," and finds that approach helps her listen to what God wants her to do.

Calling Forth Leadership

As you look for ways to serve, consider whether you have the gift of leadership, and whether that gift has been used well, is underdeveloped, or is waiting to be discovered. Perhaps leadership is not your primary gift but one that lies beneath the surface to help in other areas. Maybe you have the gift of mercy or hospitality or any one of a dozen other gifts and can help a leader get things done. As a civic leader said, "I think some people are *destined* for leadership in companies and communities. That requires sacrifice, not just from the leader, but from the leader's family."

In my work, I have the privilege of becoming involved with many businesses and organizations, ranging from large churches to newsrooms across the country to small retail businesses. In doing so, I always notice one thing: great organizations have great leaders, people who care about others while moving forward in their work.

Are You a Leader?

- Think beyond today. Dream big, and try new things on a regular basis. Leaders are innovators and are willing to take calculated—not foolish—risks.
- Have goals. Know what your business or organization stands for and what you want to see happen.
- Stay focused on your mission and your role in that mission. Surround yourself with people to help accomplish goals and to hold you accountable to the mission.
- Outline strategies to reach those goals. Leaders regularly step back to assess where they are, and whether they are on track. They follow up.

Knowing *what* you want to accomplish is always complemented by knowing *how* you will accomplish it.

- Spend most of your time on the most important things. Do not waste time putting out fires that are not important. This helps you accomplish more in less time.
- Understand that details matter. An interesting paradox is that great leaders are Big Picture people, but they also put time and energy into important details.
- Let others know how much you value them.
- Deal with problems and personnel issues in a fair and forthright way, and do not be afraid of a difficult discussion. Do not let problems fester.
- Learn to like change.
- Embrace new technology—or at least be informed about it. Do not stick your head in the sand and ignore advances.
- Communicate consistently, asking questions, listening, giving others the benefit of the doubt. Great leaders are not stingy with information.
- Help your team grow and develop, understanding that training is needed to help people move to new levels.
- Delegate, and do not try to do *everything*. Trust employees and coworkers to help move projects forward, but follow up to make sure important plans are on track.
- Set aside time for reflection and renewal and enrichment. Do not think that vacation days are to be forfeited. You need time away to see things in fresh ways.
- Think big.

Work on your leadership skills. Share your expertise with others. Teach a class. Mentor someone. Using the gift of leadership unleashes a powerful force for good. So you think you are not a leader? Encouraging potential leaders is a gift of its own.

The Power of Serving Through the Local Church

Many of these opportunities for leadership come at work. Some will come in clubs or organizations. However, in my view, a key commitment must be the church. Everyday people can change the world through volunteer church work. The local church can minister, serve, nurture, and teach.

This does not always mean raising your hand when a volunteer is needed. That can result in overload in a hurry. It does mean praying about how you can serve and what God would have you do, knowing there will always be more needs than you have time or energy to meet. I try to make church my first volunteer priority, with certain civic commitments next. As a result, I often am forced to turn down a community project that I find appealing. At church, I try to help in an area that uses my gifts, and I try not to overextend. My involvement helps me grow and increases my enjoyment of life. It nourishes me.

An Alabama woman described it this way: "The truth is I had no idea what was missing from life until I found it. My church family has helped me in so many ways. I now prioritize my workweek in order to protect the time I spend with them. There was a time in my professional life that I worked ten- or twelve-hour days, nearly every day, and thought nothing of coming in on my days off. My personal life ranked second—and a distant second, at that. But once I sought

God's help to get out of that rat race, my whole life was radically changed. Having a church family who cared about me so much made it easier for me to make my time with them a priority."

Another professional explained why she shaped her life outside work around involvement with a local church: "I felt it was important to give our child a strong Christian upbringing because I had seen through my mother how faith and a reliance on God would see us through any storm that might come our way. That reliance on God and on our church family grew as our lives together grew, and we weathered both good times and bad, both personally and professionally."

Money as Part of Ourselves

Beyond the gift of time, money is also needed—by churches and by many fine organizations that do the Lord's work each day. A commitment of financial resources shows where our heart is, what we believe is truly important. Because pay usually comes from our work, we are offering not only money but part of ourselves. From deep within Old Testament times, people gave according to their ability—and that meant time and money. In the early days of the church, this was one of the hallmarks of Christians: "Selling their possessions and goods, they gave to anyone as he had need" (Acts 2:45).

Throughout my adult life, I have struggled to put God first, and not money, not power or prestige, not success as defined by most of the world. Wrestling with this, I have realized that how I spend my money—including donations—tells a lot about what I believe in the deepest parts of my heart. This is an ongoing battle. A passage in Matthew sets me straight, time and again, about allowing income or anything else to come first:

> Do not store up for yourselves treasures on earth, where moth and rust destroy, and where thieves break in and steal. But store up for yourselves treasures in heaven, where moth and rust do not destroy, and where thieves do not break in and steal. For where your treasure is, there your heart will be also. (Matthew 6:19-21)

Our hearts follow our money, and we need to be sure part of our money is going to help others as Christ would.

Serve One Master

Reading on in the Matthew passage, another verse makes it even clearer: "No one can serve two masters. Either he will hate the one and love the other, or he will be devoted to the one and despise the other. You cannot serve both God and Money" (Matthew 6:24). Notice that the word *Money* is capitalized in that verse.

As always, the Bible's stories are of redemption and new beginnings. Go back to the "wee little man" you might have learned about as a child, another person who loved Money with a capital "M." Here is his story, fresh with promise for our lives:

> Jesus entered Jericho and was passing through. A man was there by the name of Zacchaeus; he was a chief tax collector and was wealthy. He wanted to see who Jesus was, but being a short man he could not, because of the crowd. So he ran ahead and climbed a sycamore-fig tree to see him, since Jesus was coming that way.
>
> When Jesus reached the spot, he looked up and said to him, "Zacchaeus, come down immediately. I must stay at your

> house today." So he came down at once and welcomed him gladly.
>
> All the people saw this and began to mutter, "He has gone to be the guest of a 'sinner.' "
>
> But Zacchaeus stood up and said to the Lord, "Look, Lord! Here and now I give half of my possessions to the poor, and if I have cheated anybody out of anything, I will pay back four times the amount."
>
> Jesus said to him, "Today salvation has come to this house, because this man, too, is a son of Abraham. For the Son of Man came to seek and to save what was lost." (Luke 19:1-10)

Jesus knew the man was in the tree. He knew Zacchaeus needed the grace he offered. He reached out to Zacchaeus and changed his life—the very work Jesus came to do. We are called to do our work in this same way, with integrity, giving to the poor, and making it right with those we have wronged.

In matters of hurry and worry at work, and in listening for God's voice, I have been guilty of trying to serve two masters. I found myself pulled relentlessly. Only when I committed to trying to put God first, and following wherever that led, did I begin to understand abundant life, from the true Master's hand.

A PRAYER FOR YOUR JOURNEY

Dear God, use me in service to others, and help me make a difference for good. Help me know what to be involved in and what to walk away from. Develop my gifts so that I may be useful in this world. In the name of Christ. Amen.

Tips from Busy People

We are responsible to God and to other people.

"The word I pray that will always remain on my mind is accountability. *First and foremost we have to be accountable*

to God—we should work every day to respond to his call to serve. We must be accountable to those who come to us for assistance. We must be accountable to those who support us. We should strive to be accountable to each other. It's a circle that never ends—accountability should be a part of everything we do."

Do your part.

"I'd be less than honest if I didn't admit that there's been a significant amount of personal pleasure in my community service, though I'd like to think I've made a small difference. Seems to me that's all it takes—everybody doing a little bit and being engaged in their communities."

Chapter Ten

Renewal Time

Stepping Away to Jump In Again

Encouraging Word: *Time away from work can make you better at your job.*
Everyday Step: *Take a day off to do something you enjoy.*

The greatest geniuses sometimes accomplish more when they work less.
—Leonardo da Vinci

One of the hardest-working, most talented and caring people I have ever seen works at the church I attend. She keeps a busy schedule, but she makes time for refreshing activities with her friends and family. Her approach to life is one I want to borrow on a regular basis.

"I can't imagine not having fun in life," she said. "One of my favorite Scriptures is: 'This is the day the LORD has made; let us rejoice and be glad in it' (Psalm 118:24). Those are words I try to live by. Don't get me wrong, the stress of life gets to me sometimes, but I try to keep it all in perspective. In the whole scheme of things, the problems at work or at home are not enough to waste your time being unhappy about or, more specifically, 'unjoyful.' "

Through the years I have noticed many people working longer and harder, getting more and more stressed by their daily schedules and letting their joy erode. Frequently clients declare they can't possibly take time off. They have much too much to do. They check their e-mail while on vacation, phone the office regularly, and wonder what is waiting to implode while they are away.

Small business owners work extra hours to build their businesses. Corporate employees are asked to do more with less. Church employees and others in ministry feel guilty when they take time off. When one extraordinary event or assignment wraps up, another one slides right into its place. The hours lengthen. Time off lessens.

I can't tell you how many times people have told me it is not worth it to take time off because of the workload they face while preparing to be gone. And then they bemoan the pile of work they know they will face upon their return. Some people begin to believe they are indispensable at work—that no one else can fill in for them. That often leads to a person feeling like a victim or a martyr.

Our young granddaughter spends time at our home each summer, working us into her busy schedule of T-ball, swimming, bike riding, and Vacation Bible School. She runs and laughs and eats purple ice cream. She *knows* what summertime is about.

Perhaps many of us in the workplace could take a lesson from little Gracie.

A pastor explains the importance of renewal like this: "Through the years I have experienced times of balance and times of imbalance, and I can truly say that when I have prioritized time for recreation, spiritual formation, family relaxation, exercise, and travel, in conjunction with maintaining a relationship with an accountability partner, I have felt stronger, more effective, and a better minister, even when difficulties or multiple crises arose. The opposite is also true."

The Power of Taking a Break

As a long-time manager and consultant, I have observed that people are more effective at work when they take time off. They need a break, time to step back and get a new perspective, time to rest and relax or time to do something fun. Those who schedule regular vacations and downtime are more focused and energetic when they are at work. They are not worn out, burned out, and counting the years to retirement. They see new places and try new things. They get caught up on projects at home. They just feel better overall.

In addition, there is something about getting ready to be gone for a while that helps folks focus and mow down lingering chores. Desks are suddenly cleaner, inboxes emptied, to-do lists taken care of. Motivation and momentum overtake procrastination.

My role model for renewal is not a pop psychologist or self-help author. It is Christ himself, who always had people clamoring for his time and attention and yet made time to get away and pray and rest. The Gospels tell of these incidents in rich detail, such as this one in Mark: "Very early in the morning, while it was still dark, Jesus got up, left the house and went off to a solitary place, where he prayed" (Mark 1:35). The start of a new day. Time alone. Prayer. Try that sometime soon, and savor the benefits.

When I ask workshop or class participants what they would like to do to enjoy each day more, their answers are usually sweet, tend toward the inexpensive, and speak of the need for renewal. They include cooking, spending time with a child, meditating, laughing more, taking a walk during lunch, or praying. Weaving such things into your busy daily life can make your work more enjoyable.

"Fun plays a huge part in my life," a busy worker told me. A newfound joy has been baking for her friends and coworkers. "I love to bake and do it almost every day. I truly love bringing desserts to work or surprising my friends with them. You should see their faces when I walk in bearing a steaming cobbler or some decadent pan of brownies!"

Her enthusiasm reminded me of some of the most fun times we had in the newsroom in years past, gathering in The Usual Spot, as it was called, for a staff covered-dish meal. Those lunches evolved into a cooking competition with the best food you could imagine—and work was always a bit less hurried and worried as we broke bread together.

Exercising Your Right to Exercise

Exercise is another wonderful renewal tool (and one you may need if you take up workplace potluck lunches!). "It is important to get over that hump where exercise is like work," one person told me. He starts each day with a workout, having made it into a habit.

Another busy employee believes that exercise has improved her life immensely: "About fourteen months ago, I was sitting at my desk at work, in the throes of what for me were overwhelming changes, and I said to myself, *This job is going to kill me if I don't do something to help me feel better about all these changes and handle the increased workload and stress.* I did not feel much joy or happiness with myself because I was so stressed and consequently took it out on my family or coworkers."

She joined a fitness center with a trainer, whom she calls her "fitness angel." "I really advocate getting a program and getting the right advice from a trainer," she says. "I also advise sticking with it even though it may be weeks or months before you see physical results. Almost immediately I felt better—more energetic, and I have a smile on my face ninety-nine percent of the time."

For others, a simpler approach works—but it still involves getting up and moving. "I find a good long walk is my best medicine. It will clear my head, and I will be in a better mood when I return," one businessman, who travels a lot, said.

Never Too Busy to Take a Walk

Few things energize me more than a great walk or a good run, and yet I too often let that vanish when I get busy at work. When I make this a priority in my morning routine, I lose weight, gain energy, and am less stressed. In addition, early walks are inspiring, as they offer a chance to pray or brainstorm. I feel a closeness to God, and a sense of optimism about the possibilities of the day. Writing this book has reminded me of the need never to be too busy to take a walk and never to be too busy to pray. Thankfully, the two work very well together—and they are better and cheaper than an extra shot of espresso with a cappuccino. However, they do not just happen.

More Ways to Unwind

- As you consider ways to enjoy your work more, come up with a plan to get moving. If you have been sedentary for a while, ask your doctor to tell you what you are capable of doing at this time. Don't try to run a marathon in the first month or commit to exercising two hours a day, seven days a week. Start at a level you feel comfortable with, and see what happens.

- Leave work behind when you are at home. Enjoy your evenings and weekends—take time to sit on the porch or take a short trip, read a good book, or play at the lake. Shift gears, slowing your brain down a bit and not thinking about what you *should* be doing. Avoid being always on the job in your mind.
- Think about your attachment to technology and how you might unwind by being unwired for a while. Part of this might, once again, be tossing the cell phone for a while or turning it off when you are off duty, something to help you listen to others and your inner voice or to hear a bird's song or children's laughter more often. On vacation recently, I very deliberately left my phone at home for two full weeks. That simple step was harder than I expected—but I relaxed not having to keep up with it or answer it along the way. "When I decided to retire—or as I like to call it, 'redirect,' " one executive said, "I made a vow to myself that I would not have a cell phone for at least a year. I've started my own business, and my home answering machine does the job for me. No more talking on the cell while driving or rushing to meetings. Now I'm 'in the moment' in my personal, professional, and spiritual life. Oh, what a joy it is to experience the calm and really feel God's presence in all his creation!"
- Get up early and enjoy the beginning of a new day. This is a quiet, renewing time of day, perfect for contemplating needed changes.

- Delete a handful of activities from your calendar—just for a month, as a start. This will be hard. Take away things that drain your energy or keep you from focusing on your priorities.
- Add something fun or enriching to your schedule. Go to an early movie or have lunch with a friend. Attend a class at church or volunteer to help with a children's program. One businesswoman tries to have one "Smell the Flowers Lunch" a week. "My mission for that one hour is to do anything that advances my commitment to myself to 'live a big, brave, sacred life, on my own unique spiritual journey.' " She came up with that personal mission, by the way, at an annual retreat she attends.

Family Time Is Revitalizing

Spend time with your family. Most people tell me this is a top priority, but they somehow never get around to it. Not doing it becomes a double drain. You wind up feeling guilty and stressed because you are not honoring your priorities. And you miss out on the fun of being with your family, at ease and off duty.

No wonder Christ said the kingdom of heaven belongs to children. They are so genuine and innocent, and they look at life with such wide-eyed wonder. They trust us to do right by them. Remember these words as you shape your family time: "Jesus said, 'Let the little children come to me, and do not hinder them, for the kingdom of heaven belongs to such as these' " (Matthew 19:14).

If family renewal time matters to you (and it matters to most of us), make it happen.

"This 'fun' is something I am very intentional about sharing with my children. Through their young years I have learned that putting a little extra energy into the little things will be what they remember," a busy mother said. "Do you remember the tooth fairy coming to your house? Mine will . . . her name is 'Flossie.' I know they'll remember our family vacation to Disney World, but they'll also remember the scavenger hunt they had to go through to find out we were going. Picnics in the den, antics at Christmas, making time to play games, the list goes on and on!"

Regular family activities provide fun and rejuvenation. "Sundays tend to be family time in my household," said one father who struggles to balance work and home. "We attend church and spend most of the day together."

As the seasons fly by, many people talk of the day when they will slow down or of their longing to do less. They meet themselves coming and going and miss the enjoyment of each day. Try it again. Keep at it until it begins to work in your life. Tweak. Prune. Put your feet up. "I see people around me all the time with good careers who have no fun," said a finance professional. "Someone has to make the call to friends to set up dinner, trips, hunts, golfing, etc. I try to be that person. God gave us life to enjoy and as a gift. Who receives a gift and has no fun?"

Another way to renew is to get out of your routine, which helps break habits. Changing the rhythm of your life can help you decide what gives you energy and what drains your energy and can recharge your battery. You do not have to buy a plane ticket or spend lots of money—although, use those frequent-flyer miles if you have them! Invite an acquaintance to lunch and try a new restaurant; or volunteer in a neighborhood you seldom visit; or try out a city park or swimming pool or library. Sign up to teach a class at church.

Read something challenging. Say yes to something that stretches you.

Create Each Day as a Work of Art

Consider your life as a masterpiece. How do you want it to look? How does renewal time fit into this picture?

Start with simple ways to renew each day. Make up your mind to enjoy today. Don't worry about yesterday. Don't fret about tomorrow. Enjoy today.

"It is one thing to have particular circumstances that make you sad or sorrowful but not unhappy or without joy," a friend said. "If things are such at work or home that you can't have fun or humor, then it's time to change something. I don't think God ever intended for us to just 'muddle' through our days. I think Christians should have a joy about them that should make others say, 'I want what he or she has.' "

Think about things you want to do in your lifetime—and what God wants you to do. Let your imagination soar. These range from places you want to visit to something you want to learn. Pick one to start on soon. Give thanks for each day.

Simplify your plans so you can know yourself better and discern what renews you.

Allow time for your own reflection, renewal, and worship of God. "Every morning I set aside time for prayer and reflection," a worker told me. Prayer, meditation, Bible study, and reading are ways she recharges her batteries.

Enjoy nature. Get outside more often. Observe the seasons.

Read. Keep a stack of reading material by your bed. Carry a book with you regularly. I love to see someone reading their Bible in the waiting area at the doctor's office or the car-repair shop. A pocket-sized New Testament easily fits into a purse or briefcase and can help you renew in a matter of minutes.

Time for Vacation

Those who maintain balance take vacations. "It is critical that people take time off to recharge and renew and spend personal time away from work," a business owner said. "We make it clear when we hire someone that it's expected that they will take all their vacation time each year."

How can you make time for a vacation when you feel you cannot possibly squeeze out a day, much less a week or more?

- Take advantage of June, July, and August. While summertime is not the slow season it once was, it still is a time when most children are out of school and many people plan vacations. Clients and customers and employers know that people are more likely to be in and out during these months.
- Plan for time off. Put it on your calendar in advance. If you say you'll take vacation when you have a lull, you will never get around to it. This appointment and that will soon fill up your weeks.
- If you cannot imagine taking a full week off, start small. Plan two or three long weekends. If your business is cyclical, plan an afternoon off each week during the slower times—or, better yet, take each Friday off.
- Weave days off around heavy work times. If you have a big load at work that wears you out, plan time off when that wraps up. Follow busy, intense

periods with a peaceful vacation, exploring new terrain on a trip or enjoying being home.

Retreating for Renewal

Another possibility is a retreat—either alone or with a group of people. When I encounter balanced people, I often find they take retreats every year, and sometimes even more often. It turns out that these times away are planned well in advance, and they serve as opportunities to temporarily leave behind daily responsibilities and a demanding schedule.

When I was a teenager, a retreat was something you did with a group of church friends, a bunch of sleeping bags, and the knowledge that you would come home tired. As a busy working adult, I've realized the value of a good retreat to refresh and renew. One very effective businessman I know has taken an annual silent retreat for the past ten years or so. "I will go for as long as I live and am able to go," he says. "It is the most energizing thing each year, getting beyond trials and tribulations and focusing on what is important."

Having attended and led dozens of retreats over the past couple of decades, I offer a handful of observations:

- Identify your expectations. Do you crave time to ponder your life or perhaps hear an inspirational speaker? Choose a retreat accordingly.
- Retreats can work for individuals and for groups of any size. Within the past few months I have spoken at two retreats—one was a large group of church women and the other was a medium-sized group of business leaders. While vastly different, each had a similar goal—to step back from the daily fray and gain a new perspective.

- If you want to take a personal retreat, start planning now. If you wait until you think you have time, it probably will not happen.
- A one-day retreat can be effective if more time is not available. You might take a day for prayer and spiritual contemplation or to reflect on a specific topic.
- The most useful retreats have breathing room built in. If the schedule is jammed too full, you return exhausted.

A step beyond a retreat is a sabbatical—time away for work, study, rest, or travel.

Our senior pastor took a six-month sabbatical after much prayer and planning. "During the sabbatical I traveled with my family to familiar and unfamiliar places. We shared many experiences we will never forget and developed relationships with people from different countries and different cultures. I took the opportunity to teach a class at a seminary, to live for a while in a monastic community, and I worked on hobbies, the yard, and being a husband and father. While I was gone, I developed a new appreciation for the uniqueness, creativity, and possibilities present in the congregation I had left behind. I returned refreshed in many ways and with a different horizon of awareness—no longer as enmeshed in the day-to-day details of congregational business but better able to look with fresh eyes and lead from a point of balance."

As your busy work schedule unfolds, consider time away—to take a fresh look at your life or work, away from your daily routine. Maybe this will be as simple as a play date with your child or dinner with your spouse. Maybe you will attend a retreat and explore yearnings you sense. Perhaps you will take a vacation or an extended break.

Take the plunge. Become better at work by becoming better at play. Expect pleasant surprises as you live with joy in the work you do.

May you be renewed in life and work—and do what God asks of you.

A PRAYER FOR YOUR JOURNEY

Dear Lord, thank you for giving me so many ways to enjoy each day. Help me be renewed and refreshed and to live with joy. Forgive me for letting life rush by too fast to savor your blessings. Help me have fun as your child, always. Amen.

Tips from Busy People

Create a life outside of work.

"My total sense of self had become enmeshed with my career. It took years for me to understand that this was happening, and that it was damaging my life. I had no life outside the office. I can remember crying out to God and asking him to help me separate my sense of self from my career once and for all, and he answered that prayer. He has been so faithful."

Fun at work is important.

"If I'm not having fun in my work, then at home I'm not being who I want to be. My office is fun, our meetings are fun, we socialize some together and laugh a lot together. We have to be serious enough in life, there's no reason work can't be and shouldn't be fun too."

Study Guide

Let us not become weary in doing good, for at the proper time we will reap a harvest if we do not give up.
—*Galatians 6:9*

Hurry Less, Worry Less at Work can be used for individual reflection or group study. This study guide is intended to help you consider your own life and how work can help you be the person you were created to be. If each of us can do this, we can change the world. The study tools in this guide revolve around prayer, reflection, and Scripture.

Using the book's ten chapters as an outline, the guide provides for each chapter:

- A key point to consider
- A reflection on a Bible passage
- Study questions
- A step to take in the week ahead

This study helps readers incorporate biblical teachings into everyday life and look for ways that God's words affect daily actions. The study will help you learn more about the Bible and explore modern day issues with ancient wisdom.

Incorporating renewal time into daily life is one way to hurry less and worry less at work, and this study guide can help you start a habit of prayer and reflection. In addition, groups can use the questions for discussion.

This study invites participation, but it also focuses on each individual's journey and is suited for a diverse group. Each of us is uniquely created, and we are at different places in our work lives. This means that responses to the questions may be very personal and may vary greatly. This study also can help a group develop as a community. It can help individuals discover the next steps on their journey. It is suitable for Sunday school, adult Vacation Bible School, or a small group.

Suggestions for Individual Study

Busy people find personal study time very helpful—and hard to get a handle on. I hope this book will get you started or take your quiet time to a new level. No matter how busy you are, do not let that paralyze you. Keep looking for ways to tackle the hard issues of work and home, knowing solutions will come your way. Listening for the voice of God yields all manner of blessings. As we learn to enjoy our work more, we can serve the world more energetically and live with true joy. Developing or refining the habit of prayer, reflection, and Bible study can help you grow spiritually—and help you approach work in a calmer and more contented manner.

The study questions in this guide can direct your quiet time. Consider using a journal or notebook as you move through the book, jotting down ideas and considering how God might be speaking to you each day. Many of those interviewed in these pages said that answering questions about work priorities proved quite meaningful. Perhaps you will find that true also. Using my journal as a tool helps sort my thoughts—and gets me back on track when I overload. A journal is a great place to list blessings each day, to plan a goal for that day's work, or to write a prayer.

If you are in a place of hurry and worry, it may be hard to find time for individual study. Do not be discouraged. Look for a few minutes here and there, until you discover a rhythm that works for you. As you pursue this, you will find it is well worth the time—and, thus, easier to fit into your busy life. One approach is to read a chapter and consider what it says to you. Pray about it. Ask God to give you wisdom and discernment, to use the book to help you grow. If this is your copy of *Hurry Less, Worry Less at Work*, do not hesitate to mark it up. I have an entire shorthand for making notes on what speaks to me in a book—something I want to remember, an "aha" idea, an inspirational quote, or a reference to a scripture I need to study.

My prayer is that this guide will lead the way to an ongoing prayer and study time in your life. If you falter, try again, and ask God for help. God cares about each detail of your life and has a plan just for you.

Start or Join a Small Group

As you try to find ways to grow in your busy life, turn to a faith community. Maybe you are already a member of a church but need to seek a small group or class. This can help you connect with others who struggle with issues similar to those in your life. In recent years, I have been blessed to be a part of two very different small groups, each filled with loving strangers who became friends along the way. They have been caring, sharing, and prayerful and have enriched my life.

Maybe you have been searching for a place to get to know people and ask questions about Christ. Perhaps your work is draining, and you long for others to share the journey. Take a look at a church's newsletter or website. Even if you are not a member of a church, you can participate in such classes.

Call the church office for more information, or ask someone you know.

Perhaps you are already a member of a small group and are looking for a study that will speak to a varied group of people. Maybe you have felt called to start a group and have noticed a handful of people in your congregation who might need a place where they can go deeper in their faith.

Remember: You do not have to be a preacher or Bible scholar to lead a small group. You simply have to help pull the group together, encourage others, and depend on the Holy Spirit. If you feel called to lead a group, then prepare for each class, and read the material in advance. Jot down an agenda for the meeting to keep you on track, and use notes as needed. Notify members where you will be meeting and when. While it is important to encourage people to talk, do not try to force anyone. Pray each week for an awareness of God's presence in the midst of your group. Trust that God will guide you. This class is not about you. It is about helping others learn to live more abundantly, nourished by God's grace.

Reminders for Group Leaders

Having taught many classes now for busy people, I have learned that shorter classes, which start and end on time, are helpful. While you do not want to rush through the class, keep an eye on the clock. Do not cut speakers off, but keep the discussion on track. I prefer classes of an hour or two in length. Some groups like to meet for two or three hours.

This book can be used as a ten-week study with one chapter for each week or as a six-week study, starting with an introductory discussion and covering two chapters in each of the following weeks. It can also work for a Vacation Bible

School class. A suggested approach for four nights would be to cover the introduction and the first two chapters on night one; chapters 3 through 5 on night two; chapters 6 through 8 on night three; and chapters 9 and 10 on night four.

Encourage participants to read the chapters in advance and to consider how God might be speaking to them. Ask them to pray for the class and for what they might learn or offer to others. When groups come together to talk about God's guidance, each person brings something different and wonderful to the group.

If possible, make your meeting space more personal and comfortable. You might add a candle or a cross or an item that is symbolic of the week's discussion. Perhaps someone in your group may want to help with this.

Be available to greet people when they arrive, and remember that some people are shy and even uncomfortable when they first join a group. While some members of the group may have been in your church for years, others may be new to the church and feel as though they do not fit. Helping these people feel comfortable is a precious way to show the love of Christ.

Most of the groups I lead provide some sort of refreshments, because we like to meet and eat. You might ask people to volunteer to bring snacks.

Open each session with prayer, asking for God's presence in guiding the discussion. Allow people to share in the conversation, but avoid making it seem as though someone *has* to speak. I am an Extrovert with a capital "e," but many people in my classes consider themselves introverts who like to absorb and be present, but who prefer not to talk. Remind your group that your discussions should be considered confidential. And make sure that each person has pen and paper available for taking notes.

A Sample Session

- Open with prayer and casual conversation, and provide time for chatting as participants settle in.
- Direct participants to "Going a Step Further," below, using this as an outline for the class. Ask if anyone has comments or questions on discussions from previous meetings.
- As the meeting begins, focus on the main scripture for each chapter.
- Begin your discussion with the "Key Point to Consider."
- Lead the group in reading and discussing the reflection / discussion questions.
- In each chapter, ask group members to choose a step they will take during the coming week, and invite them to reflect on their thoughts during the course of the week.
- Mention which chapters should be read before the next meeting.
- You might want to invite prayer requests as the session ends. Pray for God's guidance as each class member seeks to follow God's will.

Going a Step Further: Reflection / Discussion Questions for Groups or Individuals

After reading each chapter, reflect upon the scripture identified in the study guide, turn to the "Key Point to Consider," and ponder what it means in your life. Use the reflection / discussion questions to go a step further and help you sense how God is leading. Sometimes one question will lead to a discussion that takes you into the next, or a particular topic will jump out at you. Let the Spirit guide you to spend time as needed with these questions and to reframe them to be most effective. Individual needs within a group can be powerful in shaping discussions.

Each chapter ends with a "Focus on Growth," a step you might take to make changes in your life or to deepen your faith. This is a step that you identify and commit to take, custom-made to help you move forward with joy. Remember that God is calling you to do something special with your life, something unlike anyone else. God wants you to live abundantly and enjoy the work you do. Each person is different, so ask what God's will is for *your* life and work—and what steps you might take to be transformed in your faith and enjoy your work more. Pray about your answers, and let God shape your life.

Chapter 1

Too Much Work, Too Little Time: Learning to enjoy each day more

Key Point to Consider: We can become more effective at work, fretting less and listening closely for God's guidance. This can bring more joy to our lives.

Reflect on the Scripture: "I have come that they may have life, and have it to the full" (John 10:10). What does this verse say about how we are to live our daily lives?

Reflection / Discussion Questions

1. Chapter 1 focuses on the importance of stepping back to assess work on a regular basis. How might doing this help you?
2. In what ways do you need to trust God with your job?
3. Consider how God might want you to adjust the big picture of your life. Write down a few thoughts about this, or even just one or two words that come to mind.
4. What obstacles do you encounter when you attempt to change a busy schedule? What might you do to overcome those?
5. What does success look like to you?

Focus on Growth: Write down your big picture for your life. Pray each day for God's direction in your work.

Chapter 2

The Importance of Priorities: Making daily decisions

Key Point to Consider: Decide what is most important in life, and make wise decisions based on those priorities.

Reflect on the Scripture: "I know that there is nothing better for men than to be happy and do good while they live. That everyone may eat and drink, and find satisfaction in all his toil—this is the gift of God" (Ecclesiastes 3:12-13). What does this passage have to say about the jobs we fill?

Reflection / Discussion Questions

1. Chapter 2 points out that we sometimes stumble because we do not pay attention to our priorities. How have you handled this issue in your life? How do you deal with priorities? How do you avoid stumbling? How do you recover when you stumble?
2. What do you need to quit focusing on so much?
3. What might you trim from your schedule?
4. Many people wrestle with conflict between work and home. How have you experienced or avoided this conflict? What are some ways you might handle it better?
5. Have you lost sight of the joy you once got from your job? If so, how can you regain that joy? If not, what steps have you taken to maintain joy in your work?

Focus on Growth: Identify a top priority, along with one step you will take to honor that priority in the week ahead. Pray for discernment.

Chapter 3

God's Guidance: Being led to the right place

Key Point to Consider: God calls us to use our gifts in special ways and guides us to the right places.

Reflect on the Scripture: "Whatever you do, work at it with all your heart, as working for the Lord, not for men, since you know that you will receive an inheritance from the Lord as a reward. It is the Lord Christ you are serving" (Colossians 3:23-24). What do these verses say to you about your efforts at work?

Reflection / Discussion Questions

1. Chapter 3 mentions how things fall into place in our work. Have you experienced this in your life, and if so, in what ways? Have you had times when things didn't seem to fall into place? If so, how did that affect you?
2. Do you believe all jobs can be meaningful? Explain your answer. How does this relate to the work you currently do?
3. What part has money played in your work decisions? How do you deal with the issue of money?
4. Even if you generally are pleased with your job, some days work can be especially hard and not much fun. What are some strategies you could use to help yourself on those days?
5. Consider the following idea: *If you want to be happy, you need to choose work where you can serve others*. Do you agree with this? Why or why

not? In what ways do you serve others in your current job?

Focus on Growth: Grade yourself on how well you are doing your work. Pray about areas that might need attention.

Chapter 4

The Freedom of Focus: Organization brings its own magic

Key Point to Consider: Pay attention to your schedule to keep from overloading. Each commitment takes time and energy.

Reflection on the Scripture: "I will lie down and sleep in peace, / for you alone, O Lord, / make me dwell in safety" (Psalm 4:8). What comfort does this verse offer for overwhelmed people?

Reflection / Discussion Questions

1. Chapter 4 notes that overscheduling wears many people out and hurts enjoyment of work, relationships, and sometimes our overall outlook. In what areas, if any, have you noticed this in your life? Be as specific as possible.
2. List two or three guidelines you could use to make scheduling decisions.
3. Disorganization and clutter can cause confusion. Identify one area you might focus on to become more organized.
4. Procrastination saps many people's strength. What do you think causes people to procrastinate? Do

you see this in your own life? If so, in what ways? And if not, what is your method for avoiding procrastination?

5. Sometimes we feel as though we must get everything done at once. In what ways do you feel "snowed under," and what might you do to begin to dig out?

Focus on Growth: Put a block of time on your calendar to clean off your desk, clear out your e-mail, or take care of another area of disorganization. Pray as you do the chore.

Chapter 5

Course Corrections: Staying on the right path

Key Point to Consider: Fresh starts pop up in life, opportunities to step back and figure out if our lives are out of alignment, and why.

Reflect on the Scripture: "Whatever is true, whatever is noble, whatever is right, whatever is pure, whatever is lovely, whatever is admirable—if anything is excellent or praiseworthy—think about such things. Whatever you have learned or received or heard from me, or seen in me—put it into practice. And the God of peace will be with you" (Philippians 4:8-9). What might this passage say about how you act at work?

Reflection / Discussion Questions

1. Chapter 5 says that our lives sometimes get out of balance. In what ways have you felt this?
2. How can you tell when you need to make a course correction in your life?

3. Sometimes we know what to do but do not do it. Are there areas of your life where this is true? If so, describe them. What do you want to do differently?
4. List a professional goal you would like to accomplish in the next year. What steps can you take to accomplish this goal?
5. Identify a topic you would like to learn more about and list three ways you might begin to increase your knowledge in that area.

Focus on Growth: Identify, pray about, and implement a change to bring your life into alignment.

Chapter 6

Saying No to Negativity: Choosing a positive attitude

Key Point to Consider: A positive, Christ-centered attitude helps us handle challenges at work.

Reflect on the Scripture: " 'Love the Lord your God with all your heart and with all your soul and with all your mind.' This is the first and greatest commandment. And the second is like it: 'Love your neighbor as yourself' " (Matthew 22:37-39). What do these two great commandments mean in your workplace?

Reflection / Discussion Questions

1. Chapter 6 mentions that negative thinking can drain our energy and keep us from doing our best. In what areas, or in what ways, do you need to try to be more positive?

2. Sometimes working with other people is difficult. What steps might you take to be more loving with those you encounter?
3. Having a faithful spiritual life can help you deal with work crises. What is one building block for faithfulness?
4. Sometimes we say things that are unkind or unnecessary. How likely are you to let hurtful words come from your mouth, and how can you better control your tongue?
5. What positive impact can you have on the people around you?

Focus on Growth: In the next week, resolve to be a better listener to someone in your workplace, and pray for God to help you be aware of needs in those around you.

Chapter 7

The Busy Seasons: Managing the toughest times

Key Point to Consider: Especially busy times need to be approached with intense focus, extreme prayer, and agile planning.

Reflect on the Scripture: "I am the true vine, and my Father is the gardener. He cuts off every branch in me that bears no fruit, while every branch that does bear fruit he prunes so that it will be even more fruitful. . . . Remain in me, and I will remain in you. . . . If a man remains in me and I in him, he will bear much fruit; apart from me you can do nothing. . . . This is to my Father's glory, that you bear much fruit, showing yourselves to be my disciples. . . . You did not choose me, but I chose you and appointed you to go and bear fruit—fruit that will last. Then the Father will give you whatever you ask in my name" (John 15:1-2, 4, 5, 8, 16). How might God be speaking to you through this passage?

Reflection / Discussion Questions

1. Chapter 7 shows how circumstances can cause us to be extra busy. How can you deal with an extremely hectic time at work?
2. Sometimes personal matters complicate our work lives. When this happens to you or those around you, what could you do to ease the situation?
3. List and reflect on / discuss what you are thankful for in the most frantic of times.
4. The Bible tells us to cast all our cares on God. Name a handful of cares you need to turn over to God.
5. In what areas of your work must you show self-control?

Focus on Growth: Be alert to activities that threaten to overload you, and pray that God will help you with your calendar.

Chapter 8

New Territory: Trusting God with big questions

Key Point to Consider: God goes before us as we venture into each day and into changes in our work.

Reflect on the Scripture: "I pray that out of his glorious riches he may strengthen you with power through his Spirit in your inner being, so that Christ may dwell in your hearts through faith. And I pray that you, being rooted and established in love, may have power, together with all the saints, to grasp how wide and long and high and deep is the love of Christ, and to know this love that surpasses knowledge—that you may be filled to the measure of all the fullness of God" (Ephesians 3:16-19). What do these verses say about Christ's power in our lives?

Reflection / Discussion Questions

1. Chapter 8 says we will be blessed if we follow God's directions. In what ways have you seen or thought about this in your own life? Do you ever struggle with this promise, and if so, how?
2. Fear may accompany changes at work. In what ways might you be fearful as you think of the future? How can you move beyond those feelings?
3. Is change affecting your life? In what ways? How can you adapt to changes?
4. How difficult is it for you to get out of your comfort zone? Do you ever sense that God is nudging you from one place to another?
5. What words of encouragement would you offer someone going through a time of transition?

Focus on Growth: Seek God's guidance in the timing of changes. Pray, asking God to help you know when to stay put and when to jump in.

Chapter 9

Time, Talents, Money, Mission: Giving something back

Key Point to Consider: We are called by God to be good stewards of what we have been given. That means we must always look for ways to offer something back to our world.

Reflect on the Scripture: "Do not store up for yourselves treasures on earth, where moth and rust destroy, and where thieves break in and steal. But store up for yourselves treasures in heaven, where moth and rust do not destroy, and where thieves do not break in and steal. For where your treasure is, there your heart will be also" (Matthew 6:19-21). How does this passage speak to you and your use of time and money?

Reflection / Discussion Questions

1. How important is it to be involved in our communities and churches? How do we juggle this with other priorities?
2. In what ways might you be uniquely qualified to serve as a volunteer?
3. Sometimes we must say no to a worthy cause, especially in busy seasons or times of life when we have extra responsibilities. How might you turn down a worthy request when you are overloaded?
4. Why is it sometimes difficult to give money to good causes? How can a person decide how much and to whom to give?
5. In what ways can we show that God is the master of our lives?

Focus on Growth: Identify the volunteer cause you feel most strongly about, and pray about how God would have you serve.

Chapter 10

Renewal Time: Stepping away to jump in again

Key Point to Consider: People are more effective at work when they take time off for rest and renewal.

Reflect on the Scripture: "This is the day the LORD has made; let us rejoice and be glad in it" (Psalm 118:24). How does this verse relate to your daily work life?

Reflection / Discussion Questions

1. How important is fun in your life? What is one way you could add more fun to each day?
2. What renews you and gives you energy?
3. Do you need to detach from your cell phone or computer for a break? What could keep you from doing so? What small steps will help?
4. Recall a fun vacation or break from work in your past. What made it special?
5. Who is someone you would like to spend more time with? How might you schedule that?

Focus on Growth: List three things you would like to do for fun, and plan time to do them. Ask God to help you step back when needed and to give you the peace that goes beyond understanding.

The following may be used as a handout and given to each group member as the meeting wraps up. For an electronic version, e-mail judy@judychristie.com.

Too much work, too little time:
What's a person to do?
7 steps to less hurry, less worry
(Choose one each day and focus on it)
By Judy Christie
"Hurry Less, Worry Less at Work"

Do not conform any longer to the pattern of this world, but be transformed by the renewing of your mind. Then you will be able to test and approve what God's will is—his good, pleasing and perfect will. —Romans 12:2

1. Pray and reflect upon what God wants your life and your work to look like. ("Speak, Lord.") Figure out what you need to do to make it look like that. Make decisions accordingly.

2. Get the basics of your work under control. Keep a good calendar. Jot your to-dos down in one spot, not on a scrap of paper here, a napkin there. Know where to find stuff on your desk. Meet your deadlines. Don't procrastinate. Allow extra time on the front end, so you're not rushing at the last minute. Start meetings on time. End meetings on time. Take advantage of small amounts of time to get things done.

3. Focus on your priorities. Keep the big picture in mind. Remember that saying no to one thing is really saying yes to something else. Pick your spots wisely. You cannot do everything. For everything you gain, you may have to give something up. Let some things go. Solve nagging problems.

4. Set boundaries on scheduling, and handling work and volunteer matters. Establish a flexible routine, with a goal for when you go to work and when you leave, or when you start work on a volunteer project and when you stop. Take a lunch break or an afternoon stroll. Consider the ebb and flow of your life, the season of time you're in, the flow of activities. Plan your schedule with this in mind.

5. Plan reflection/study/renewal time. ("Be still and know that I am God.") Keep a journal. Exercise.

6. Do fun things, things you really enjoy.

7. Rest.

Tell Me Your Story

I would love to hear about your journey and how God is at work in *your* work.

E-mail me at judy@judychristie.com. For ongoing tips on living fully, go to judychristie.com. Do not forget: God created you for wonderful things. Enjoy today!